TRANSGENDER, INTERSEX, AND BIBLICAL INTERPRETATION

SEMEIA STUDIES

Steed V. Davidson, General Editor

Editorial Board:
Pablo R. Andiñach
Fiona Black
Denise K. Buell
Gay L. Byron
Masiiwa Ragies Gunda
Monica Jyotsna Melanchthon
Yak-Hwee Tan

Number 83

SBL PRESS

TRANSGENDER, INTERSEX, AND BIBLICAL INTERPRETATION

by

Teresa J. Hornsby and Deryn Guest

SBL PRESS

SBL PRESS

Atlanta

Copyright © 2016 by SBL Press

Library of Congress Cataloging-in-Publication Data

Names: Hornsby, Teresa J., 1959- author. | Guest, Deryn, author.
Title: Transgender, intersex and biblical Interpretation / by Teresa J. Hornsby and Deryn Guest.
Description: Atlanta : SBL Press, 2016. | Series: Semeia studies ; Number 83 | Includes bibliographical references.
Identifiers: LCCN 2016019417 (print) | LCCN 2016020103 (ebook) | ISBN 9781628371352 (paperback) | ISBN 9780884141563 (hardcover) | ISBN 9780884141556 (ebook)
Subjects: LCSH: Transgender people—Biblical teaching. | Gender—Biblical teaching.
Classification: LCC BT708 .H676 2016 (print) | LCC BT708 (ebook) | DDC 220.8/306768—dc23
LC record available at https://lccn.loc.gov/2016019417

Printed on acid-free paper.

Contents

Abbreviations

AB	Anchor Bible
ABD	*Anchor Bible Dictionary*. Edited by David Noel Freedman. 6 vols. New York: Doubleday, 1992.
AOAT	Alter Orient und Altes Testament
AOTC	Abingdon Old Testament Commentaries
AUSS	*Andrews University Seminary Studies*
BAR	*Biblical Archaeology Review*
Berit Olam	Berit Olam: Studies in Hebrew Narrative and Poetry
BibInt	*Biblical Intrepretation*
BibInt	Biblical Interpretation Series
BibOr	Biblica et Orientalia
BJS	Brown Judaic Studies
BMW	Bible in the Modern World
CBC	*Children's Bible in Colour*
GNB	Good News Bible
GCT	Gender, Culture, Theory
GLQ	*GLQ: A Journal of Lesbian and Gay Studies*
HSM	Harvard Semitic Monographs
IDB	*Interpreter's Dictionary of the Bible*. Edited by George A. Buttrick. 4 vols. New York: Abingdon, 1962.
JBL	*Journal of Biblical Literature*
JNES	*Journal of Near Eastern Studies*
JQR	*Jewish Quarterly Review*
JSNTSup	Journal for the Study of the New Testament Supplement Series
JSOTSup	Journal for the Study of the Old Testament Supplement Series
JSS	*Journal of Semitic Studies*
JTS	*Journal of Theological Studies*
KJV	King James Version

KTU *Die keilalphabetischen Texte aus Ugarit.* Edited by Manfried Dietrich, Oswald Loretz, and Joaquín Sanmartín. 3rd ed. Münster: Ugarit-Verlag, 2013.

LHBOTS Library of Hebrew Bible/Old Testament Studies

Mx. Mixter

NCBC New Century Bible Commentary

Neot *Neotestamentica*

NIBCOT New International Biblical Commentary on the Old Testament

NICOT New International Commentary on the Old Testament

NIDB *New Interpreter's Dictionary of the Bible.* Edited by Katharine Doob Sakenfeld. 5 vols. Nashville: Abindgon, 2006–2009.

NovT *Novum Testamentum*

NovTSup Novum Testamentum Supplements

NRSV New Revised Standard Version

OBT Overtures to Biblical Theology

OTL Old Testament Library

SemeiaSt Semeia Studies

SHBC Smyth and Helwys Bible Commentary

Signs *Signs: Journal of Women in Culture and Society*

TDOT *Theological Dictionary of the Old Testament.* Edited by G. Johannes Botterweck and Helmer Ringgren. Translated by John T. Willis et al. 15 vols. Grand Rapids: Eerdmans, 1974–2006.

UCOP University of Cambridge Oriental Publications

VC *Vigilae Christianae*

VT *Vetus Testamentum*

WBC Word Biblical Commentary

ZNW *Zeitschrift für die neutestamentliche Wissenschaft*

Introduction: The Body as Decoy

Teresa J. Hornsby

We are Internet-dependent here in the first world. It is where we get the morning news and updates on the personal and professional goings-on of friends and colleagues around the world; we learn about beer making, new music, and real estate deals; we watch films and listen to music; we read film reviews, book reviews, and stay connected with recent scholarship in all the varied academic arenas in which we work. It is disparate and chaotic, unstructured, without boundaries, and, simply put, a hot mess—and we like that. Our brains move seamlessly from fermentation processes to musings on life, the universe, and everything.

It was on Facebook that I came across the video clip from Katie Couric's 2014 interview with Carmen Carrera and Laverne Cox (Rude 2014). After asking Carrera pointed, invasive, and personal questions concerning her trans surgical[1] procedures, in order to "educate those who are not familiar with transgender" (and by the way, if someone wants to be "educated" about the surgical procedures or any of the hormonal regimens, Google it—it is all there), Couric turned to Cox with the same line of questions. Cox began by telling Couric about the lived experiences of trans people: that discrimination and violence occur disproportionately in the trans community when compared to other demographics. For example,

---

1. Throughout this volume, there is a deliberate space between "trans" and other terms, such as "surgical," "people," and "man." The decision to do so is informed by Julia Serano (2007, 29), who argues that merging such terms reinforces that there is an unmarked "man" (or person, community, etc.) of which "transman" is a variant, "without ever bringing into question … assumptions and beliefs about maleness and femaleness." If trans studies are to problematize and call into question such assumptions, then our grammatical terminology needs to facilitate that. Having said that, we make two exceptions throughout: we use the terms "transgender" and "transsexual" primarily because we are following the designations of our sources.

in the United States, one in twelve of all trans persons will be physically assaulted (one in eight if you are a trans person of color) (Dunbar 2006). According to the National Coalition of Anti-Violence Programs' 2012 report (NCAVP), this rate is one and a half times larger than nontrans lesbian/gay/bisexual (hereafter LGB) persons (cited in Rude 2014). In addition to the constant threat of physical violence, the attacks on transsexual persons are, predictably, economic. According to key findings of the 2009 report of the National Center for Transgender Equality and the National Gay and Lesbian Task Force, in the United States, transgendered people have double the rate of unemployment than the population as a whole, 97 percent of the 6,450 respondents reported harassment on their jobs, and 15 percent exist below the poverty level, at an income of less than $10,000 per year (cited in Rude 2014).

After reciting some of these statistics to Couric, Cox then shared the story of the murder of Islan Nettles, a trans woman of color who was beaten to death on August 17, 2013, and whose killer was set free. Cox told Couric (and us) that the public's preoccupation with genitalia and the physical aspects of transition "objectifies trans women and distracts from the real issues." She goes on to say, so eloquently and directly, that trans people are looking for justice, and "by focusing on bodies we don't focus on the lived realities of that oppression and that discrimination" (Rude 2014). This is a critical point: Is she saying that by focusing on physical bodies, we cannot attend to how those bodies are treated in the real world? Is she saying that by focusing on *specific* parts of the body (genitalia, eyes, hands, etc.) we are not doing justice to the whole body? Is she saying that specific body parts become a diversion that pulls the public's attention from the social constructedness and the social reception of the whole body? We do not mean to speak for Ms. Cox, but we would answer yes to all of these questions.

The bottom line is this: the complexity of bodies and their social destinies are all entangled within (and produced by) heteronormativity: the dominant belief system that relies on fixed and binary genders and the certainty that heterosexuality is the norm that occurs naturally, that is, apart from cultural influences. All other sexual relationships are deemed culturally produced (unnatural), are regulated and defined in relation to heterosexuality, and are thus devalued. In this system, females and males (whose bodies are produced *naturally*) are assumed to be the only appropriate sexual partners. Heterosexism, then, is a systematic social bias that stems from heteronormativity in which society rewards heterosexuals (in the form of economic benefits and civil rights) and punishes all other sexualities.

Closely related to heteronormativity, heterosexism would be the way that a heteronormative worldview is manifested within social contexts. If one assumes that heterosexuality is the norm, that it occurs naturally or that it is divinely blessed or sanctioned, then one also assumes that those persons who identify as heterosexual would receive more benefits, rights, and rewards and would be looked upon favorably in general. Everyone, then, who does not claim to be heterosexual is perceived and treated as a second-class citizen and is discriminated against in every level of social encounter (legal, medical, religious, psychiatric, etc.).

At the institutional level, heterosexism is evident. Even though the Supreme Court decision *Obergefell v. Hodges* in June 2015 legalized same-sex marriage across the United States, the full legal ramifications of the decision are yet to be worked out. Key issues such as adoption, custodial rights, hospital spousal rights (if hospitals give power of attorney or decision-making power to closest relatives, the same-sex partner can be excluded from visitation or critical health-care decisions), inheritance, and rights of survivorship to shared property are still uncertain. This uncertainty is particularly pronounced in areas where federal rights intersect with religious institutions (a same-sex couple may be able to adopt from the state, but can they adopt from Catholic Charities?). Even as marriage equity has won its day in court, sexual orientation is not a protected class, and therefore it remains perfectly legal to discriminate against LGB people in housing and employment in most cities and states.

Like sexism, racism, or classism, heterosexism depends upon the assumption that there is a "normal" (thus superior) way of being (divinely ordained and/or "natural"). Those who view themselves to be in the "better" of any of the previously mentioned binaries usually do not see the privilege society grants them—they may assume that those in the lesser binary do not deserve the same rights and privileges (this seems to be most evident in racism and in heterosexism), or they are ignorant (or in denial) of their own privilege.

Though at first glance it may seem that "heteronormativity" and its subsequent heterosexism are not explicitly bound to trans issues, on the contrary, heteronormativity with its dependence upon an artificial framework of only two, naturally occurring sexes (as determined by genitalia) is the lynchpin that holds together all of the justifications of the violence and discrimination that is placed upon trans bodies.

The intense amounts of violence and economic punishment are "logical" extensions of a belief that the trans person's gender is "fake," because it does not occur "naturally" and is not connected to the sex that the trans person was born with (Serano 2007, 13). Thus, according to a dominant heterosexist/cissexist ideology, transsexuality is unnatural, deviant, and against God's order, which therefore removes divine blessing and, in some instances, sanctions violence against it. Julia Serano points out that this belief that a gender is inauthentic if it cannot be connected to one's sex is naïve. She writes, "We make assumptions every day about other people's genders without ever seeing their birth certificates, their chromosomes, their genitals, their reproductive systems, their childhood socialization, or their legal sex. There is no such thing as a 'real' gender—there is only the gender we experience ourselves as and the gender we perceive others to be" (2007, 13).

If the power of heteronormativity resides in its unquestioned status of "normal" and its unchallenged place at the foundation of a sexuality that is "good" and "blessed," the buttress of the whole façade is Bible translation and interpretation. Only in recent times (the last few decades) have scholars initiated a critique of the heterosexism that permeates all Bible reception at least since the nineteenth century. The burgeoning field of queer biblical studies has produced compelling scholarship, which seeks to show the heteronormative biases that punctuate biblical interpretation. For example, as one reads Genesis, apart from the example of Rebekah and Isaac, where does one actually find one man married to one woman? Apart from the purity codes of Leviticus, where does one find a clear condemnation of homoeroticism in the Hebrew Bible? How should one understand the place of Ebed-melech (Jer 38:7), an Ethiopian eunuch (intersex perhaps) who rescues Jeremiah and is blessed by God? Or, as we explore here, what can one make of Jezebel's masculinity? Can we read Gen 1 in such a way that "the monstrous other" is indeed part of, not apart from, the Creator?

A prominent (and dominant) reading of the relationship of God to Israel (and later, Christ to the church) is one of husband and wife, the groom and the bride. Yet, ironically, as queer readers point out, the "people" of Israel and the "church" refer to "men" (as are God and Jesus). Thus, if one holds on to that metaphor of marriage, both examples are *same-sex* marriages. As postmodern readers of the Bible suggest, the reader makes meaning. Heteronormativity is not *in* the text, waiting to be discovered; the interpreter or reader brings the assumption of heteronormativity to the text and uses the text to justify heteronormativity.

Like the air we breathe, heteronormativity, heterosexism, and cissexism are pervasive yet invisible; it is an assumed and unquestioned notion that there are only two naturally occurring and opposite sexes and that each is, naturally, attracted to the other. This heterosexual desire is created and blessed by a deity. These assumptions then dictate that there are only two genders. Hence, any and every expression of gender that does not "match" one's assigned physical sex is rendered deviant; any sexual desire not directed to one's opposite sex is aberrant. This aberrance is interpreted as sin or as unnatural, which justifies punishment and violence against sexual and gender "queers."

Heteronormativity is a culturally produced ideology, justified and maintained institutionally through religious beliefs, economic and political systems, medical classifications, psychiatric diagnoses, and judicial processes. The dominant premise of heteronormativity permeates every detail of someone's life: love, marriage, aging, death, reproduction, property ownership, leisure time, and every single other thing. Only in recent times has the "natural" occurrence of heteronormativity been challenged, and with this recognition has come a chipping away of the mighty fortresses of heterosexism. Through academic studies of heterosexuality and through the visibility and increased activism of those considered nonnormative by the dominant ideology, more and more are questioning the presumed natural, divinely blessed, and normal status of heterosexuality.

But as some of the sexual and gender queers move toward the center (finding some social acceptance through heteronormativity), the trans person is "the Other's Other." Those who live a gender that is different from their birth genitalia or those who change their physical sex to match their lived gender can find few allies. To some queer theorists, the idea that one is "born" a particular sex (regardless of genitals) and that one's existing physical body must be altered to "match" the internal chemistry of one sex or the other flies in the face of the counteressentialist notions of gender upon which queer theory rests; gender is a socially constructed entity with no "essential" tie to physicality. Here it is necessary for gender theorists to recall Jay Prosser's (1998, 84) reminder of the importance of the materiality of the body. Though the lived gender may be more or less aligned with one's physicality, the performed masculinity or femininity lives out a subversion that maintains queerness; it is masculinity or femininity with a difference. A transsexual (one who opts for surgery) can do it in a quieter way (than posttranssexual activists such as Sandy Stone or Kate Bornstein, for example) that acknowledges the comfort gained from body/gender alignment while also acknowledging a trans history.

To a general Christian laity, the body is as God made it, and sex and gender are inextricably bound. In this mind-set, to alter one's God-given genitalia is "unnatural" and, in lay terms, sinful. Thus the trans person has no advocate here. What we offer in this volume are alternative readings of foundational Bible texts that refuse to pit order and chaos against one another (ch. 2) and show that any sexed body can perform any gender (ch. 1).

Additionally, there is no haven, particularly for the male-to-female (MTF) trans person, within radical feminism. We see an emerging and continuing transphobia, particularly as it is presented in the work of Sheila Jeffreys, Julie Bindel, and Janice Raymond. Jeffreys (2005, 53–58) understands MTF surgery as a reiteration and tragic reproduction of impossible, misogynist, and oppressive standards of beauty for women. In *Transsexual Empire: The Making of the She-Male*, Raymond (1979) describes transsexual surgery as an invention of the medical industry for profit. Bindel (2004) claims that transsexualism reinforces the notion of gender essentialism. She writes, "I don't have a problem with men disposing of their genitals, but it does not make them women, in the same way that shoving a bit of vacuum hose down your 501s does not make you a man." In the same vein, Elinor Burkett (2015), writing in response to a media frenzy caused by Caitlyn (née Bruce) Jenner's public statement that her brain is more female than male and that femininity is expressed primarily through fashion and "feminine" emotions, states that

> [MTFs'] truth is not my truth. Their female identities are not my female identity. They haven't traveled through the world as women and been shaped by all that this entails. They haven't suffered through business meetings with men talking to their breasts or woken up after sex terrified they'd forgotten to take their birth control pills the day before. They haven't had to cope with the onset of their periods in the middle of a crowded subway, the humiliation of discovering that their male work partners' checks were far larger than theirs, or the fear of being too weak to ward off rapists.

From that critical perspective, Jeffreys, Bindel, Raymond, and Burkett do have a point: there are experiences that women-born-women have endured throughout their lives that are part of a shared identity. Yet does this reduce the category of "woman" to one of victimhood? Perhaps that reduction is, in light of historical realities, appropriate. Does this then require that we claim that "the oppressed" is a feminine category?

Again, this does seem to be another historical reality. This line of feminist ideology reflects the productions of power that Michel Foucault (1978) describes: sex is invented to produce and keep power in place. Moreover, as Judith Butler (1990) asserts, "sex" is produced by an imaginary gender binary. If "feminine" is reiterated as "oppressed" and "weak" in feminist discourse, it is an example of the production of the category "woman" that seeks to thwart a dissolution of gender boundaries (which are, ultimately, the foundation of all power). In other words, all misogyny rests upon the (usually well-intentioned) impulse to define "woman."

In that reiteration of the gender binary, where does that leave the autonomy and personhood of one who chooses to physically transition? That oppression then becomes attached to her new body. Radical feminism here misses the point: in its defense of women-born-women (another category of "woman"), radical feminists overlook the source of villainy— misogyny—which is maintained by the two-gendered system. If such a system were not in place, if the categories of "male" and "female" were allowed to dissolve, the "protection" of the category "woman" would not be necessary. By defending the category "woman" at the expense of those who are in fact dissolving the binary, we are defining (confining) women; the two-gendered system is reinforced. The phobia that radical feminism places upon the bodies of trans women is simply misogyny in different clothing. As Deryn Guest writes later in this volume,

> the road to transsexuality *does* subvert supposed coherence between sex and gender. It disturbs, it unhinges expectations, and it prompts violence. But once the chosen gender is inhabited, do we lose that sub- version because the person occupying it is pressured to demonstrate that their sex and gender are congruent? No. The lived femininity (or mascu- linity) is a different femininity. (ch. 3)

As gay and lesbian cissexuals are enjoying more social acceptance (as witnessed in recent same-sex marriage legislation in the first world), it has come at a cost of creating (or, rather, solidifying) the transgendered person as "other." The "acceptable gays," those who have become models for human rights issues (such as marriage, adoption, and nondiscrimina- tory practices in employment and housing) tend to be men and women whose lifestyle mirrors heterosexual monogamy. As gays and lesbians find a place in the church, the church's message tends to be, "We accept you because you are 'good' like us," rather than, "We accept you just as you are because you are a child of God." The trans person is excluded. We are reminded of a punk anthem, "Domesticated Queer":

> There is no fucking diversity
> No victory over hate
> No tolerance or acceptance
> We just assimilate
> Thought we had it all
> But lets be sincere
> All that we've become
> Domesticated Queers!
> You know they're gonna love you
> Cause you're just like them!
> You know they're gonna love you
> Cause you're just like them!
> You know they're gonna love you
> Cause you're just like them!
> You know they'll fuck you over
> Cause you're just like them.
> Say we pick our battles
> So we can win the war
> Someone please remind me
> What the hell we're fighting for?
> Go tell that little faggot
> No high heels at the polls
> Too queer to be here
> We just want your vote[2]

The lyrics reflect the quasi-acceptance of the trans person as a means to a political end but not much acceptance beyond that. Trans people become an unwanted other at many LGB "family friendly" events.

The trans person becomes the lightning rod, because he or she makes a private struggle public. On a fundamental level, the trans person's battle is about personal autonomy. Neither queer theory, nor fundamentalist Christianity, nor radical feminism gives the individual the power to choose a sex and/or gender for oneself. Queer theory posits that culture determines gender, which usually remains a binary; Christian fundamentalists posit that God determines the sex, which therefore determines the

---

2. "Domesticated Queer." Words and music by Rebecca I. Doss, 2014. See http://www.c-rex.com/#!about/guq4k.

gender; and radical feminism sees the production of gender as an extension of power, that those who hold fast to gender stereotypes are collaborators in the oppression of women. It seems to us that Bible scholarship has a unique role to play here—one that empowers the individual to live fully in his or her chosen (or rejected) gender and/or sex.

So, to revisit Cox's assertion that attention to the trans body diverts us from the real issues, I would say this: attention to the trans body is *good* if it is indeed the *whole* body. Rather, what we witness, as far as trans bodies are concerned (and indeed, the bodies of all *others*), is a hyperfocus on body parts (usually the genitals); those parts then are allowed to represent the entire person. If the social body is intellectually dissected, with hyperattention paid to the genitalia, we cannot be surprised that the public is unable and unwilling to accept the full humanity of the trans person. As we note in chapter 3, that body becomes "monstrous." More, the rhetorical violence upon the body desensitizes the public to the material and real violence that follows.

Definition of Terms

Already in this short introduction, we have used words that may not be familiar to many readers. For example, *cissexuals* are simply those who present and live a gender that is the same as the one with which they were assigned at birth. Serano (2007, 12) defines the corresponding term *cissexism* as "the belief that transsexuals' identified genders are inferior to, or less authentic than, those of cissexuals (i.e., people who are not transsexual and who have only ever experienced their subconscious and physical sexes as being aligned)." Thus cissexuals experience some social privilege that trans people may not. As with heterosexism (and racism, classism, and sexism), privilege is invisible to the dominant group, and basic privileges are denied to the "lesser" group—in this case, noncissexuals (transsexual/transgender persons). Since Western social arrangements depend upon *heteronormativity* (there being two, and only two, sexes that occur naturally), cissexuals' privilege tends to occur on a more personal level (in addition to institutional biases).[3] To some this may seem to be a trivial matter, but, for example, transgendered persons are often denied equal access to public restrooms or department store fitting rooms. However, this ostensibly slight discrimination is critical for this reason: all of

---

3. For a discussion of "heteronormativity" and "heterosexism," see page 84.

Western culture stands upon a two-sex system. The one way this system is concretized (made "real") is through the separation of the physical, naked body in public space (restrooms and dressing rooms). If there is any intrusion into the fantasy of a "two sexes and two genders" system, the center cannot hold. It is no coincidence, then, that violence against trans persons is extraordinarily high, which appears to be connected to the very high occasion of suicide attempts. Cox's (and our additional) statistics above attest to all the ways that a culture, whose existence depends upon heteronormativity, will punish those who fail to do their gender right.

You may have noticed that we are not using words such as *transsexual*, *transgendered*, *queer*, or *genderqueer* in reference to a trans person. We are not opposed to these terms in general, but we are choosing to use the descriptor *trans* simply for its inclusivity *and* its specificity. We find that with the addition of *sexual* or *gender* to *trans*, people assume that we are making a distinction between those who physically alter their bodies and those who have not. Furthermore, many of us have worn the clothes of our nonbirth gender since we could choose for ourselves. So at what point does one consider oneself to be "transgendered"? Is it only at the point that one senses a social aversion directed at her or him or *them* (a pronoun that is often preferred in order to eliminate the binary)? Regardless of what may or may not be concealed under one's clothes, trans people still experience the same social attitudes.[4]

We are also not using the term *queer* to describe trans people. Though an inclusive concept that serves as an umbrella for persons who do not fit neatly into a category (which is, of course, everyone), "queer" is too broad. While all trans persons could be included in the grouping "queer," not all queers are trans persons. Trans persons receive disproportionately greater incidence of discrimination and violence. There must be a more specific descriptor for this distinct group toward which so much social hatred is directed. There is a much more nuanced discussion of these terms in chapter 3.

CISSEXUALS WRITING ABOUT TRANS PEOPLE?

We, the authors of this volume, are white, and we receive all of the privilege that society bestows upon our race. We are academics, which sug-

---

4. For a discussion of how and why Guest specifically models a trans gaze and not a transsexual gaze, see ch. 2.

gests that we enjoy a certain amount of class privilege as well. Some of this privilege is lessened because we are women, and a portion of that privilege is also reduced by being visibly *queer* women. Yet even in our queer female bodies, we do not experience the same terror that our trans friends are likely to encounter each time they enter a strange place or walk down an unfamiliar street or attempt to use a public restroom. We (mostly) do not fear being fired from our jobs or being refused housing. We are fairly certain that if we are violently attacked, the assailant will be prosecuted and sentenced. Despite the clear privilege that we enjoy in our presumed cissexuality and the corresponding lack of empathetic understanding for pressing trans issues that we may have as a result, we choose to write what we hope to be something that moves us toward social justice and civil rights for trans persons; movement, in a good world, would lead to acceptance, love, and celebration.

This volume, *Transgender, Intersex, and Biblical Interpretation*, is itself a bit queer in that it is a collection of essays by two authors, yet it should be read as an integral unit. While each chapter can be a stand-alone essay, our claim is that biblical narratives have been read and continue to be read through a gender-binary lens with heteronormative bias. In each chapter, we offer an example of how paradigmatic narratives are radically transformed when we read without the assumptions that go along with that binary and acknowledge the presence of ambiguously gendered subjectivities. Deryn Guest "troubles" the binary in chapters 2 and 3 by rereading Gen 1 and the Jezebel-Jehu encounter in 2 Kgs 9–10, respectively; Teresa Hornsby reassesses King David's dance in 2 Sam 5–6 and the Christian Apocalypse in chapters 4 and 5, respectively. In a concise description of what we are doing in this volume, Guest writes in chapter 3 that "applying the trans gaze to biblical texts is a vital new hermeneutical lens that can offset the heteronormative ends to which biblical texts are often put and provide a counterdiscourse to those who use the Bible to denounce transgender or transsexual persons." In short, we are trying to undo the heteronormative way in which biblical texts have been read and used; we are both using the lens of trans theory to interpret texts in new and illuminating ways; we are both committed to the ethical imperative to do this given the way Scriptures can be mobilized for transphobic purposes; and we are both working toward more inclusive curricula for the field of biblical studies. These are the perspectives and goals that unify the constituent chapters and hold the book together.

1

GENDER DUALISM, OR THE BIG LIE

Teresa J. Hornsby

I had a total knee arthroplasty (total knee replacement) a while back. After abusing my knees through sports, compounded with genetically programmed old-lady arthritis, my new knee is a breath of fresh air. Another breath of fresh air was my surgeon. My initial meetings with him were so frustrating—he was *always* running late. I learned to take work or my iPhone with me to kill time. Then I realized the reason he was always so late was because he is a "chatty Cathy": talk, talk, talk. My "consultations" with him eventually became long conversations about the development of the prosthetic knee, which I found fascinating. It turns out that the bioengineering of knees has gone through a long evolution; in the decade of the 1970s alone, there were more than thirty prototypes due to the introduction of methyl-methacrylate, a polyethylene plastic (Hamelynck 2010). The first mechanisms were one size fits all; it was up to the surgeon to fit the patient to the knee replacement. Eventually, doctors were given a greater range of product sizes in order to fit the knee to the patient—small, average, and large. However, "average" tended to refer to the "male" knee, though it turns out that 70 percent of total knee replacement patients are women. While some argue that a "gender-specific knee" is marketing hype, some clinical reports claim that there are gendered differences, that the male knee is broader (Greengard 2012). Male prosthetic knees are referred to as "standard," and female prosthetic knees are referred to as "narrow," even though most knee replacements are for women (would one not refer to the "female" knee as "standard" and the "male" knee as "broad")? Nevertheless, my surgeon tells me that there are primarily two companies who insist on marketing gender-specific knees, Zimmer and Biomet, and that he and his colleagues ignore the gender designation. In his experience, a surgeon simply finds the knee with the best fit. Despite marketing efforts to designate body parts into two, and only two, genders, the material fact is that, at least in the case of the knee joint, body parts are not gender specific.

None of us should be surprised at this information. Gender, like everything else in the world, emerges like a prism. One is neither one gender nor another but maybe one of thousands on a scale; moreover, even if one identifies as, let us say, hypermasculine *today*, this does not mean that that particular gender is set. Events taking place through the years, months, even days may produce a newly determined gender performance. The evolution of the knee replacement mechanism is an odd but concrete example of culture (via marketing) attempting to create a dichotomy where there is not one: there is simply no physical category of either male or female; the trans body is a material fact. While many are willing to accept that gender is culturally produced and articulated through things like hairstyles, clothing, or mannerisms, many still cling to the notion that somehow our genitals make us either a man or a woman, regardless of which gender we may perform. In short, the trans body is not a minority exception to a two-gendered system; it is not an anomaly or a body that exists in the margins. The reality is that there are no margins. The trans body is a material manifestation of the gender illusion writ large. As Virginia Ramey Mollenkott writes, "Far from being a mere tagalong to gay, lesbian, and bisexual liberation, transgender liberation is absolutely central to the entire movement" (Mollenkott and Sheridan 2003, 39). Mollenkott rightly recognizes, as she refers to Margaret Atwood's *Handmaid's Tale,* that those who defy gender norms are considered to be our worst criminals and are punished as such. What is the terror, the repulsion, the monstrous that a populace associates with the trans body?

More than a few years ago, I was channel surfing during daytime television. Running the midday gamut of soaps, reruns of old shows, and, of course, talk shows, I landed on the train wreck called *The Jerry Springer Show.* I stopped there because there was yelling, anger, and indignation from the audience toward one lone individual. I had never heard such vitriol, even on this blight of a TV show. I had to know: what had this individual done to incite the crowd to such heights of hatred? Grandmother rapist? Child molester? Flag desecrator? No. This person simply refused to reveal "his" or "her" gender. People were furious, screaming, "You know you're a man! Say it!" or "You're a woman! You know it! Say it!" This was astounding to me, and it revealed, as Mollenkott observes, that Westerners have a deep-seated transphobia, a base fear of gender fluidity and instability. I found myself searching that televised body for clues: Hair style? Clothes? Stubble? Body language? I remained perplexed but not angry. I guess it is obvious now, but the degree of anger the audience unloaded on this person made no sense to me. It seemed so disproportionate. Jerry Springer prides himself on presenting the most despicable situations and people and in creating a frenzied blood-in-the-water response from the spectators. Yet I think even he was surprised at the venomous contempt in the room toward someone who had no victim, a person who simply would not be confined by a gendered either/or.

A person such as this, one who refuses to submit to an arbitrary two-gendered existence, is indeed a dangerous person—a threat to the raw power that rests entirely upon the lie of a binary gender paradigm of two—and only two—opposite sexes. Springer's audience knew this on some level. I suspect none of them knew *consciously* why they hated that intersex or nongendered person or why their anxiety reached a feverish pitch. But phobias erupt this way; they emerge from a culturally produced fear that that which is stable and secure is about to become unstable and dangerous. The trans person, by by her, his, or their mere existence, is proof that gender is dynamic, unstable, and culturally constructed; the trans person is a testimony to the absurdity of a natural and static gender. This threat to power's foundation is precisely why the trans body is targeted for violence, and, as every trans person knows, that violence is often justified through selective interpretations of biblical texts.

Literal and traditional/historical Bible exegeses have "confirmed" for most that, indeed, God made humans in that way—in two distinct and opposite genders. Conservative Christians read Gen 2:18–24 in just this way, that God, from the beginning, established "complementarity" by creating one man and one woman. The gender pairing is reiterated in the new creation story of Noah, as God plans to repopulate the destroyed earth (Gen 7:1–3). Both these texts, especially Gen 2, have a deep and troubled history of interpretation. The story of the first humans is where fundamentalist Christians draw the line in the sand. For this reason (the centrality of the creation stories of Gen 1–3), we begin with Genesis, though we are certainly not the first to deconstruct previous and grandiose interpretations that rest (so precariously) on that creation myth.[1]

---

1. See "Homosexuality and Biblical Interpretation" (n.d.) for a rudimentary over-

Even if we know nothing else about gender, its construct, and its ubiquitous presence, we can *look around* and *know* that it is simply not true that there are only two, opposing genders. Just as Paul writes in Rom 1:20: "Ever since the creation of the world his eternal power and divine nature, invisible though they are, have been understood and seen through the things he has made."[2] In *Omnigender: A Trans-religious Approach*, Mollenkott (2001) talks about the realization of her own transgenderedness. She explains it in such a way that it is for us, as it was for her, an extraordinarily surprising "Aha!" moment. Surprising in that we have studied gender a very long time, and we have acknowledged the social constructedness of it, and we have thought and talked about trans issues and the liberation of gender from the body. But, as she writes, "Even when I was arguing that the Bible supports male-female equality … I was unable to lift myself free of the confines of gender duality" (xi). She goes on to say that through, in part, Leslie Feinberg's description of some masculine women being forced to wear feminine clothes, she remembered (as do we) how "foolish, unattractive, inappropriate, and humiliating" it feels to wear clothes that do not fit our gender (though socially "appropriate" to our genitals) (xii). As a young "tomboy," having to leave my jeans and PF Flyers aside while I wore my frilly dresses to church seemed grotesque. Like Mollenkott, it took decades of my own "cross-dressing" to finally realize, in a personal way, what it means to be transgendered. Most of us, some more than others, present ourselves as a gender that has no place. It is not an either/or, it is not stable, and it is not what society expects of us.

After her profound insight into her own gender identity, Mollenkott develops a theology, firmly anchored in scriptural and church traditions that imagine (or rather, preclude) an "omnigendered" society. Mollenkott understands that the two-gendered system is an unjust one and thus requires a social justice theology that comes to the aid of those "gender outlaws"—or rather, gender transcenders, which, in reality, are most of us. Mollenkott's "trans-Christianity" embraces the gender fluidity that she finds in a number of emblematic Christian passages: the birth of Jesus and Mary's virginity; the interactions of Jesus with Mary of Magdala and with the beloved disciple in John; and finally in Paul's transformation of a com-

---

view of how many conservative Christians understand the Genesis text. Though shoddily researched and documented, it is a good example of the exegesis that is used to argue the "natural thus normal" existence of two—and only two—opposing genders.

2. Unless otherwise stated, all translations of biblical texts follow the NRSV.

munity that is "neither male nor female." For Mollenkott, Christianity is, at its very essence, an omnigendered, flexible, and *trans*formative entity. She writes, first quoting an unpublished work of David Herrstrom,

> "John insists with Jesus that the act [of following Jesus] frees 'you' into more life in this world, breaking down the walls between tribes, genders, and classes; and in the next as well, erasing the threshold between life and death." It is this category-transcending, passionate, and compassionate vision of the human face divine that will stimulate and sustain our attempts to achieve omnigender justice. (Mollenkott 2001, 211)

Justin Tanis, who self-identifies as a transgendered male, sees *trans*formation as being fundamental to Christianity as well. Tanis (2000) looks to the account of a "Canaanite" woman who begs Jesus to heal her daughter (Matt 15:21–28) to make several points: (1) God's goodness is for everyone, regardless of social status; his following analogy is especially gripping: "This woman approaching Jesus to help her daughter was like a drag queen approaching a bunch of teenagers on a street corner for change to call 911 after her sister has been beaten" (45); (2) those who are in need of help, or who are in the margins, must be relentless in their demands for justice; (3) with a clear sense of self, one can confront power; finally, and most critical, (4) power can be transformed, and confronting power is transformative. Tanis writes, "Looking at Jesus as the one who was transformed from using epithets to healing has helped me to remember that the name caller today can be the ally of tomorrow" (51). This final point is critical, because it leads down the same path that Mollenkott leads us: Christianity is meant to be transformative. It is, as Tanis writes, a counter to "a vision that sees the world only in terms of two genders and one way of living in it" (52). This narrow vision

> misses the totality and beauty of creation. Christ is an alchemist. If we affirm that Jesus lived as he died, then his life must also be a story of alchemy, transformation, and resurrection.... As people of faith, we are called to transform ourselves and our world. A transforming, learning, growing Christ is one who can guide us through that process of change. (52)

One cannot claim with certainty "this is the *real* meaning, or the *truth*," but I would venture to say that a trans hermeneutic gets closest to what may be essential in Christianity: fluidity, dynamism, inclusivity, and transformation.

A trans hermeneutic grasps the essence of a living, breathing, dynamic Christianity and finds a representation throughout the Christian Scriptures. For example, Victoria Kolakowski (1997a, 40) claims that even though the Bible has been used to support notions of modern marriage and sexuality, there are always exceptions to those antiquated laws that allowed "people's needs to be met when circumstances did not quite work as required under the rules, particularly when those fictions served the social purposes underlying the rules." She looks specifically at accounts of eunuchs and claims that they were of "ambiguous gender" and would fall within the sexual category that we would today broadly call "transgendered" (42). She goes on to say, "As a result, many of my transgendered sisters look to the ancient eunuchs for affirmation of our history and spirituality" (43). We see in Kolakowski's trans readings of Jesus's remarks about the eunuchs and the kingdom of heaven (Matt 19:12) and the story of the eunuch whom Philip converts (Acts 8:26–40) that she is resentful (rightfully so, it seems) that gays and lesbians have hijacked the biblical eunuch as one of their own. She claims that trans folks are second-class citizens in the gay and lesbian community:

> A growing number of gay and lesbian Christians are correctly embracing the image of the eunuch as a liberative one, although most of them are simultaneously ignoring the fact that it is only by analogy that it applies to them. Many of these same gay and lesbian Christians are embarrassed by, or are otherwise uncomfortable with, transgendered people, and hence try to distance themselves from us.... This results in a form of cultural hogging of tradition, which denies to transgendered people our own history and which marginalizes us. (48)

Kolakowski sees the biblical eunuchs as a shining, subversive symbol— subversive, because they refuse subsumption into the two-gendered, procreative system. She reads eunuchs as a powerful and positive portrayal of trans characters, over and against Janice Raymond's view of eunuchs as castrated men used to infiltrate women's spaces and to control women. For Raymond, trans women are castrated men who have acquired women's artifacts; they cannot be "unmanned," meaning that they still hold on to all of the privilege that society endows upon the phallus (Kolakowski 2000, 110).

Kolakowski also reads against Nancy Wilson's rendering of eunuchs, which claims that eunuchs are all equal in God's eyes and that they have been used as instruments of God (e.g., 2 Kgs 9:30–37). Kolakowski seeks to find a middle ground between Wilson's co-option of the eunuch as gay and as part of God's plan (who does indeed, à la Raymond, destroy the strong woman) and Raymond's desire to banish the trans woman from female space (Kolakowski 2000, 110–11). Kolakowski ultimately concludes that the trans woman must find her own way as she exists in the "in-between." She can neither be banished from "women's space," nor can she be fully assimilated into a "women only" existence. She knows that biblical texts (and for Kolakowski, particularly ones about eunuchs) can be used to both support and undermine trans liberation and community building.

Of course, trans people have been reading the Bible all along, looking for themselves, looking for those who represent the reality of gender transcenders. Indeed, they are there in those texts. Trans folks understand that the notion that there are only two and opposing genders, intent toward reproduction, is ludicrous. They (we) also know that to expose such a false foundation to all that is sacred is dangerous. Gender is the absolute bedrock (rock bottom) of all civilization. I am not exaggerating here. Those who are intersex or who refuse to claim a gender or who live another gender from that which society has assigned based on an imaginary "two-sex" system are living proof that gender and sex are an illusion. The problem is that all power structures stand erect upon that foundation; when gender falls, everything falls. How then can one live a life of civilized normalcy, one that has an ethical component and is an extension of a traditional belief system, when one's own lived life guts that system? What follows here is a blueprint. It is a blueprint that draws from the creation of the world in Gen 1, from Jezebel's feminine masculinity, from King David's dance, and from Jesus's defiance of social norms. In the end, we offer this: a Scripture-based rebellion against the two-gender lie. Clearly, materially, biblically, nothing is either/or.

2

TROUBLING THE WATERS: תהום, TRANSGENDER, AND READING GENESIS BACKWARDS

Deryn Guest

The opening verses of Genesis are dramatic, perhaps best imagined as a theatrical opening. Picture the stage production: curtains pull back to reveal only impenetrable darkness. The audience strain their eyes but nothing comes into focus, even though the audio speakers around the auditorium indicate something is there—it laps, perhaps ominously, perhaps menacingly, perhaps indifferently. Some primordial stew of fluidity lurks. But what is this? A detectable low sound of another presence, brooding, hovering, maybe the stirrings of wings or a wind whirling up. Then pupils swiftly contract, the audience rapidly shade their eyes and turn away, as a divine injunction suddenly floods all with light.

Full of interpretational possibilities and describing a nonworldly scene hard to imagine, it should not surprise anyone that commentators find it difficult to grasp fully what is going on in Gen 1:1–3. The remaining verses are less challenging. Step by step, the Deity produces a world of binaries: night and day, waters above and below, and, at the pinnacle of creation, a foundational binary pairing of man and woman, divinely ordained, to inhabit an earth that has been established with fauna and flora. The speech-acts that occur in this chapter both perform and enact. Thus it is that the biblical narrator orders the world around him, controlling the troubling presences of his opening verses, תהום and תהו ובהו, and putting all under the splendid authority of his main character—Yhwh Elohim. Commentators who read with the grain of the text usually share the narrator's sense of wonder, seeing in this creation a wondrous establishment of order out of chaos. They reify this chapter as a grand and glorious opening, a powerful intervention by a wonderful deity. It is, writes Gordon

Wenham (1987, 40), a "triumphant affirmation of the power and wisdom of God and the wonder of his creation." Why would anyone wish to read otherwise? Specifically, why would anyone advocate reading backwards, putting the focus on those nebulous entities? Primarily because reading with the text enables facile text-proofing arguments that assume the stability of a heteronormative sex/gender system and condemn trans people to the realm of the abject.

The *abject* has been defined by Julia Kristeva (1982, 4) as "what disturbs identity, system and order. What does not respect boundaries, positions, rules. The in-between, the ambiguous, the composite." We all live as neighbors and hosts to the abject; it sits uncomfortably close, and Kristeva's evocative opening summarizes this unnerving presence:

> There looms, within abjection, one of those violent, dark revolts of being, directed against a threat that seems to emanate from an exorbitant outside or inside, ejected beyond the scope of the possible, the tolerable, the thinkable. It lies there, quite close, but it cannot be assimilated. It beseeches, worries, and fascinates desire, which, nevertheless, does not let itself be seduced. Apprehensive, desire turns aside; sickened, it rejects. A certainty protects it from the shameful—a certainty of which it is proud holds on to it. But simultaneously, just the same, that impetus, that spasm, that leap is drawn toward an elsewhere as tempting as it is condemned. (1)

Trans people do not fit into the world of Gen 1 except, I will argue, as individuals whose fluidity threatens the narrator's ideology of a God-ordained, ordered, binaried world. Reading backwards permits me to undo creation, to resist the assumptions and desires of the biblical narrator, and to find in that primordial mix a surprisingly fruitful way of reconsidering our relationship with it, one that might allow chaos a voice. The rationale for doing so lies in the need to take ethical responsibility for biblical interpretation, to question texts that make some lives unspeakable—that is, lives that are not routinely permitted to speak for themselves in theological discussions and unspeakable in the sense that those lives are often plunged into the abject.

Reading Genesis backwards reverses us from that binary pairing of man and woman to the undifferentiated "earthling" of 1:26. Feminists, such as Phyllis Trible (1978) and Carol Meyers (1988), have already highlighted how אדם can be interpreted as a neutral term, punning on Hebrew אדמה, telling us more about humanity's kinship with the dust of the earth than about sexed identities.[1] But I want to go further back to a more foundational pairing, that of creation and chaos, and examine that. My aim is to render Gen 1 less capable of being used, uncritically, in religious positional statements as a bulwark against transgender and transsexuality and to see in it, rather, grounds for the radical inclusion of those lives.[2] To accomplish this, in the first section I analyze the words used in Gen 1:1–3 to describe the formless fluidity that exists prior to the first words of God. In the second section, I introduce Margrit Shildrick's work on the monstrous, for this can help us unpack the boundaries that get erected in Gen 1. The third section applies the observations thus made to trans issues in particular, noting how existing religious positional statements are oppressive and arguing for a more mature way forward.

THE GRAMMAR OF THE PRIMORDIAL

תהום

Variously translated as the "deep," "abyss," or "waters," תהום is a key term used by the writer to evoke a primordial fluidity that has no apparent boundaries. As anyone with a household leak knows, water has the capacity to seep into the fabric of a building, oozing through plaster and brick, revealing itself in places that may be far removed from its place of entry. It can undo the boundaries of partition walls and ceilings, causing them to soften, bend, and eventually collapse under its pressure. When this is considered on a cosmic level, the threat is terrifyingly magnified. Even though biblical texts report that the Deity has them under control, these cosmic waters remain threatening. As C. L. Seow notes, once tamed, תהום can nourish trees (Ezek 31:4, 15) and give much needed water to wilderness wanderers (Ps 78:15–16). "But the waters of the deep were not always so reassuring to the Israelites. Landlubbers that they were, they found the ocean terrifying" (1992, 126).

The ability of תהום to conjure disturbance is also seen in scholarly debates concerning its grammatical form. Is it, for example, a proper noun, reflecting a time when תהום was understood as a personified chaos monster that needed to be subdued? Against the view that תהום is just an

---

1. However, note the contrary arguments in Barr 1999 and Clines 2003.

2. I provide a detailed examination of the terms *transgender* and *transsexual* in the section "Owning the Transgender Gaze" in ch. 3.

anarthrous noun, תהום has an entry in O. Odelain and R. Séguineau's *Dictionary of Proper Names and Places in the Bible* (1982). E. J. Waschke (2006, 574–75), noting two exceptions, Isa 63:13 and Ps 106:9, asserts unequivocally that it is used "as a proper name without the article" in the Hebrew Bible and cites, approvingly, Nicholas Tromp's (1969, 59) view that the word תהום retains its sense of primordial oceanic depths that "continually threaten the cosmos" and "is a vigorous and often grim word, which never entirely renounced its mythical past."[3]

Decisions appear to be connected to how far one is prepared to acknowledge the mythological connotations. Scholars who uphold the Genesis narrator as a new thinker, making a decisive shift away from the creation mythologies in his cultural milieu, seem the most strongly opposed to reading תהום as a proper noun. Roberto Ouro (1999, 50) illustrates this trend well. For him תהום "has no personality or autonomy; it is not an opposing or turbulent power." He cites Claus Westermann's (1997, 1414) claim that it is not "hostile to God, ... is not personified, and has no mythical function." תהום does not even have to be tamed. Ouro's paper rids the Genesis account of any dependence on Enuma Elish, banishes the notion of the Deity having to do battle with hostile forces, reinforces the creation of the world by effortless divine fiat, and argues that the biblical account is not demythologizing, as Hermann Gunkel (1895) argued, but is actually antimythical. The effect is to promote the biblical narrator as more advanced in his theological thinking and to endorse the narrator's rhetoric that the Deity has supreme control over all things, so much so that there are no remaining hints of resistance, either from the darkness or from תהום. In my view, it is this eagerness to detach תהום from correspondences to Tiamat that unhinges תהום from any proper noun status.

However, there are good reasons for restoring proper noun status to תהום. First is the obvious fact that apart from the two exceptions noted above, תהום appears without the definite article, and anarthrous terms are usually proper nouns. Second, in some texts תהום takes on personified action, such as Gen 49:25 and Deut 33:13, where it "crouches" below, and Habakkuk's reference to תהום "giving voice" (3:10). The crouching is suggestive of the "quasi-personal nature" of תהום, since the verb is "commonly used elsewhere of animals, including the mythical dragon (Ezek 29:3)" (J.

---

3. For a fuller discussion on the possibility of a common Semitic root for both תהום and Tiamat, see Tsumura 1989 and J. Day 1985. See also Lambert 1965, who argues against any deliberate borrowing from Enuma Elish.

Day 1985, 50). Third, given the mythological connotations in the writer's cultural milieu, which associated primordial waters with deities, it remains plausible to read תהום as a proper noun even if those connotations remain only as a bleached-out watermark in Gen 1, present only in their purposeful rejection by the narrator.

If תהום can be claimed as a proper noun, then capitalization of *Tehom* is justifiable. But תהום is a queer noun: masculine in form, yet usually appearing as a female noun, but occasionally given a masculine suffix (e.g., "his voice" in Hab 3:10). It is, intriguingly, a gender-shifting word, a fact that prompts discomfort in some commentators, as seen in Victor Hamilton's (1990, 110) attempts to pin it down. Given that תהום can cross masculine and feminine forms, one cannot readily supply a title such as scholars have done for ציון (Woman Zion) or חכמה (Lady Wisdom). Its gender shifts require a suitably blurred indicator. So "Mixter" is my title of choice. Borrowed from the vernacular of trans communities, Mixter (Mx. for short) replaces Mr., Ms., Miss, and Mrs. The Hebrew image for a fluid, subterranean watery mass upon, with, or against which God constructs the created world I will henceforth refer to as *Mx. Tehom.*

תהו ובהו

In addition to Mx. Tehom, the primordial situation is described by the word pair תהו ובהו, the primary meaning of which is difficult to grasp concretely. בהו does not appear independently; it features only with תהו in Gen 1:2, Jer 4:23, and Isa 34:11. תהו can mean uselessness or futility, as in 1 Sam 12:21, which contrasts a human king with Yhwh. It is clearly implied that the former cannot save them or bring them any profit—the king is akin to תהו, perhaps one might say "a waste of space." The term also carries this sense of futility in Isaiah's polemic against idols in 41:29 and 44:9. In other contexts, it appears to mean "nothingness" (29:21), while elsewhere it can refer to a disorienting lack of coordinates, that is, the pathless desert wherein persons might easily lose their way and die (Deut 32:10; Job 6:18). The reference in Isa 34:1 to תהו lines and בהו stones describes a situation where all the stable units of measure have been lost.

There is a general acknowledgment of the very disturbing qualities of תהו ובהו. Wenham (1987, 15, 16) speaks of the "frightening disorganization" represented by the phrase, adding that "the dreadfulness of the situation before the divine word brought order out of chaos is underlined." He sums up the phrase as "total chaos" (14). For Ludwig Koehler, Walter

Baumgartner, and Johann Stamm (1994–1999, 4:1689), it brings to mind "the terrible eerie deserted wilderness." M. Görg (2006, 570) mentions the onomatopoeic qualities of the phrase, "clearly intended to conjure up associations with something menacing." For him, "the two nouns belong to a sphere that stands in opposition to the ordered world" (570); תהו ובהו describes "not simply the 'unproductive and uninhabited place'" suggested by D. T. Tsumura (1989, 43) but "a hostile and uninhabitable environment" (Görg 2006, 572).

In my view, it is the word pair's ability to conjure something being without form, pathless, and lacking in coordinates that is most disturbing. The narrator of Gen 1 has summoned a gender-shifting, fluidic deep combined uniquely with a description of formlessness: an opening scene of eerie, evocative, nonworldly sounds and presences, all lurking in the darkness, to which we now turn.

חשך

Wenham wrestles with how we are to interpret this darkness. On the one hand, it is negative: "If light symbolizes God, darkness evokes everything that is anti-God: the wicked (Prov 2:13), judgment (Exod 10:21), death (Ps 88:13)." On the other hand, Wenham notes that "God can veil himself in darkness at moments of great revelation (Deut 4:11; 5:23; Ps 18:12)" (1987,16). Wenham's acknowledgment of the ambiguity is helpful. Is the darkness that envelops Mx. Tehom a threatening force, or does it imply a hidden presence of God?

Nicolas Wyatt (1993) persuasively argues that the darkness is a figure for the Deity's invisibility and that what we have in Gen 1:2 is a theophany. It is a strange theophany to be sure: "first, there is the seemingly improbable condition of primordial chaos in which it is to occur. Second, there is the inchoate medium of revelation: the darkness. And third, there is the spirit of God intuited rather than seen traversing waters as yet unordered" (550). Wyatt argues that תהום and תהו ובהו are also indicators of this invisibility—not, we note, of divine absence. Darkness is not necessarily something dislocated from the Deity's presence.

In summary, the opening verses of Gen 1 are difficult to translate with precision and are, indeed, perhaps more readily interpreted in the moody opening of Haydn's *Creation*. What we can say is that the terminology is eerily resonant and, above all, queer: the onomatopoeia of ובהו

תהו and its associations with a radical lack of coordinates and the gender-shifting oddities of Mx. Tehom, whose capacity to engulf the world in water is held back only by something suprahuman, all enfolded within חשך, lend the opening an evocatively mysterious atmosphere. But it is the audience that fills this opening stage set with meaning, some identifying maligned entities, some seeing forthcoming hostility and conflict, others feeling only the presence of obedient, subservient matter waiting for the divine word. Whatever the case, what is significant for this discussion is the capacity these terms have to signify the other side of created order with its light, its careful containment of creation into measurable days, its binary divisions. One is marked by fluidity, formlessness, darkness, and the absence of containment, the other by boundaries and order. The presumption is that the latter is by far preferable. But we can read the text differently, resist being willing followers of its rhetoric and explore, rather, the mechanics of that rhetoric.

To this end, what is particularly pleasing in Wyatt's (1993, 552) account is his recognition of the "constant pressure among scholars" to downplay the force of the primordial elements by seeing them as "thoroughly demythologized." In Wyatt's view, this focus on demythologizing actually diminishes the material. What we have in Genesis is a reuse of prevalent mythologies, a "twist," in Wyatt's words, on a larger collection of material (552–53). It is important not to lose sight of that. In the desire to promote the biblical writer's view as singularly distinctive, there is the implication that Gen 1 is not myth at all.[4] However, while Gen 1 is a cleverly and carefully written alternative with its own political ideology, it is still mythmaking, not something sui generis. It offers a rival mythology, a powerful alternative, but mainly a piece of political propaganda from which scholars could detach themselves a little more than is currently the case and think about how its rhetoric operates and, importantly, what it costs to hold it in place.

Fascination, Repulsion, and Boundary Making

Readers are expected to agree that the boundaries and the established order of Gen 1 are desirable and that suppression or elimination of the

---

4. Hasel, for example, refers to the "sharply antimythical polemic" of Gen 1 and to the "parting of the spiritual ways which meant an undermining of the prevailing mythological cosmologies" (1972, 20).

primordial is warranted. Yet those opening verses with their references to תהום and תהו ובהו capture the senses; they intrigue and fascinate with their mysterious connotative allure. I am reminded again of Kristeva's talk of how the abject poses a disturbing threat, yet simultaneously beckons. But another scholar whose work on the monstrous can help us unpack the boundary marking that is going on in Gen 1 and also explore the anxieties that motivate the biblical writer to evoke a deity so powerful that he can hold any threat at bay is Shildrick (2002).

Shildrick's work on the monstrous has applicability to the primordial elements that appear to be shunted outside the created realm of light and order. Discussing travel literature and bestiaries, freak shows, illustrations, and discussions of monstrous others, her work explains why the monstrous is both fascinating and disturbing. Fascination and curiosity, for example, are provoked by the radical difference and perceived unnaturalness that is on display in the freak show. The visitor is allured; compelled by a rather macabre intrigue to view bodies that are different, the visitor can nonetheless reside fairly securely in relative normalcy with a "there but for the grace of God" stability. However, disturbance cannot be warded off, and the stability of the viewer is not altogether secure, for the monstrous cannot be separated off quite so easily.

Shildrick illustrates her point with reference to the man-monkey displayed by P. T. Barnum and tales of abduction by aliens. Barnum, a nineteenth-century showman, presented a "what is it?" spectacle that featured a supposed cross between human and monkey. As they gazed upon this creature, viewers could experience, with relief, their own "normalness" in comparison with this man-monkey. However, as Shildrick points out, although this experience may have evoked "feelings of cultural and racial superiority," viewers who perceived the monkey-man as existing beyond the boundaries of normalcy had to simultaneously deal with the presentation of this creature as the "supposed 'missing link'" of human evolution (25). The man-monkey thus presented an inherent feature of our own DNA and history, and this uncomfortable recognition creates a sense of disturbance and uncertainty about ourselves.

Shildrick notes how the freak show lost respect and moral grounding, disappearing in the 1950s, but the underlying compulsion to contemplate the monstrous emerges in continuing, different ways. We see it in horror and sci-fi movies but also in stories of how human bodies are manipulated when abducted by aliens: "The apparent widespread belief—in the world's most scientifically sophisticated nation, the United States—in the putative invasion of alien beings, and their interference in the human body, speaks eloquently to the instability of both material and ideological frontiers" (25). The abducting aliens might be outsiders, but tales that tell of probing and interference with the abducted body indicate that the alien "is always both strange and external, *and* familiar, even intimate. It is the marker, then, not of the successful closure of embodied identity of the selfsame, *but of the impossibility of securing such boundaries*" (25, emphasis added).

As such, the freak show, the monstrous, offers its "gross insult" to the *ideal* of a singular, stable, unified body (10). I emphasize *ideal* to reinforce the point that the idea of stable, fixed, unified bodies is not a reality but a myth. Bodies are produced continually through repeated compulsory performances, and it is only the repetition that creates a sense of things being stable, natural, or normal. While we perceive of the "natural" as something being innately in its rightful place and uncontaminated, it is also "base and unruly—that which must be controlled—and at worst that which is deeply disruptive and uncontrollable" (11). Accordingly, the threat posed by the monstrous is not its propensity to invade or "overrun the boundaries of the proper" but the "promise to dissolve them" (11).

Dissolving, Not Testing, Boundaries

If we apply Shildrick's work to Gen 1, then we would be encouraged to consider that the biblical writer's rhetoric belies an anxiety that Mx. Tehom poses a fluid challenge to the firmament and boundaries that the Deity has established and, moreover, has the potential to dissolve them. For example, תהום is used in the Psalms to describe an individual potentially swallowed by the depths. In Ps 68:2, 15, a psalmist imagines himself overcome and pleads that תהום not be permitted to engulf him entirely (see also Ps 42:7). תהום also haunts creation in a literal way, available to return the earth to an oceanic abyss. In Gen 7:11, we read how the springs of תהום burst out or, one might translate, were cleft or split in some way, allowing the waters to pour forth. The sense is of boundaries collapsing. In Gen 8:2, these springs have been closed. Ouro (1999, 50) claims that the passive verbs in both verses "indicate clearly that the flood was not a caprice of nature, but that both its beginning and end were divinely ordered and controlled." Yes, but this bespeaks the desire of the narrator to have these waters controlled, and if he has such a desire, does it not imply that they are otherwise a menacing threat? We do not have to follow Gunkel's arguments for *Chaoskampf* to see that the threat of תהום and the desire to have it subdued entirely make the passive voice an entirely suitable grammatical and rhetorical tool to achieve this end. As it stands, the text does what it needs to: it contains the deep by putting it all under the command of a deity. But in this, we can detect the narrator's anxiety about the potential of an unclosed, bursting-out deluge, of an undone creation, and his choice of grammar marks how he chooses to hold back that anxiety. It is both acknowledged—תהום can burst forth—and controlled—תהום is closed off. The potential for catastrophe is averted, achieved grammatically in the passive voice, carefully not granting any overt autonomy to תהום.[5]

If we shift to Jer 4:23, we find a situation where the elements of precreation not only test the boundaries but dissolve them entirely. Jeremiah imagines a dystopia when an apocalyptic visit by the Deity's fierce anger leads to the earth becoming תהו ובהו, variously translated as "without form and void" (KJV), "a barren waste" (GNB), or in The Message's paraphrase, "pre-Genesis chaos and emptiness." It is precisely the lack of established pathways or boundaries, the lack of coordinates, the radical disorientating nature of formlessness, that is so very disturbing. In Jeremiah's vision, תהו ובהו is summoned at the Deity's command, so these nouns are still contained by having them under the control of God; but the terrifying thought is of a deity who surrenders the containment of these forces, which, without such limits, can reduce the earth to an original primordial stew.

However, Shildrick's insights take us further than the view that these elements test the boundaries. We are familiar with the notion that creation is founded upon the apparent banishment of these elements or the supposed taming of them, but they do not go "away." Once they have been conjured, they do not simply hold a binary in tension (creation/chaos). Rather, like the monstrous in Shildrick's work, they signify that the binary

---

5. This is consistent with a strand of scholarly argument where תהום is seen as an entirely passive element with which the Deity works. Thus, for Wenham (1987, 16), there is "no hint" that תהום "was a power independent of God, which he had to fight to control. Rather, it is part of his creation that does his bidding." Others who adopt this more passive understanding include Hasel, who argues that the narrator of Gen 1 dissociates himself entirely from cultural notions of a sea deity. In fact, there is a double-distancing rhetoric—first, תהום is not Tiamat or Nun; but second, תהום is not even a powerful other with which the Deity has to contend: "In Gn, God wills and the powerless, inanimate, and inert waters obey" (1972, 9). Ouro (1999) takes a similar line.

cannot hold; that the monstrous is already *always within* the ordered. It lurks. It coexists.

Commentators are thus right to talk about the imprint of hostile chaotic elements that is left as a faint signature across Gen 1. For example, W. G. Lambert (1965, 287) notes how Gunkel believed that "a conflict had existed in Hebrew traditions of creation, but had been washed out of the monotheistic formulation of Genesis 1." "Washed out": a watermark on a page of Gen 1 that can be palely seen, a palimpsest that nods toward the text's connections with other cultural coexisting mythologies of chaos being defeated. So while the writer of Gen 1 may well be rejecting contemporary mythological notions, he does not remove those connotations entirely. The marks of an erasure remain. Hasel (1972, 7) concedes that "cognates [of תהום] are deeply mythological in their usage in ancient Near Eastern creation speculations." Those cognates, in my view, demonstrate how glimmers of rival accounts linger, and the biblical writer's herculean effort to overthrow them is like the desperate, but ultimately impossible, attempt to cast the monstrous into a realm of the abject. The biblical writer makes his stand and his claims to the "normalcy" of his view, but the watermark remains. That it is there explains why it was so easy for a generation of scholars to embrace Gunkel's account and why feminist scholars detect the erasure of female sacral power in this text. Tiamat hovers in the peripheral margins as a rival imagining of primordial precreation waters.

FEAR, ANXIETY, AND THE CONSTRUCTION OF THE REPULSIVE OTHER

Shildrick's work further enables us to think more clearly about the damaging effects of texts motivated by boundary anxiety. She argues that we project the monstrous as "other," because this is a vital means of shoring up our own supposed normalcy. Constructing the realm of the abject provides a supposed safety and separation from what is so disturbing. Indeed, our normalcy is *dependent* upon our ability to do this. The monstrous is thus a signifier not of the abject domain but of our *normality*, or, in her words, "of a self that is constructed discursively against what is not" (2002, 29–30). An inevitable but damaging effect of creating the realm of the abject in which the monstrous can be caged is thus that the domain of the monstrous becomes pervaded with pejorative connotations.

Drawing on Kristeva's (1982, 1991) work, Shildrick (2002, 82) argues that the "emotional intensity of loathing directed at those who display unacceptable differences ... is the expression of the disavowal of the 'impure' facet of our own unconscious." In other words, because we cannot cope with our own monstrousness, we project it as "other" and load all our self-repulsion on to that "other." But, as Shildrick observes, this is a problem that could be overcome, not by repression, but by acceptance.

If Mx. Tehom and תהו ובהו were to be seen as *integral* aspects of the world, not as something that we need speech-acts of creation to subdue or displace, then perhaps this would lead to a more accepting, rounded appreciation of the forces of the primordial. The anxieties and fears that have produced the othering could be transmuted by a more mature acceptance of coexistence. This would not be tantamount to following Ouro (1999) and Hasel (1972) in their arguments that the primordial elements were putty in a deity's hands. On the contrary, this interpretation readily concurs with the narrator that these mysterious forces are threatening and frightening. But instead of the instinct to control them by creating a divine character who can put them to flight by word alone, one would consider the value of sitting alongside those anxieties, acknowledging the fears and the threat, without banishing them to an abject domain.

Shildrick emphasizes that we all have part of us located in that "outside" place and that there are no boundaries that actually have the power to separate us from what is located there: "the monstrous cannot be confined to the place of the other; it is not simply alien, but arouses always the contradictory responses of denial *and* recognition, disgust *and* empathy, exclusion *and* identity" (2002, 17). So, while it seems that the monstrous can be used to set a barrier between the "normal" and the "abnormal," it can never be "completely externalized" (55). It is by recognizing this mutuality between those who occupy the safe "normal" ground and those who are abject, acknowledging this commonality, and allowing ourselves to be a little undone that facilitates understanding and empathy.

Resolving Antipathy through Shared Vulnerability

When faced with Karl Grimes's *Still Life* exhibition, Shildrick found herself shocked by the images displayed ("many bodies with hydrocephalic disorders, exposed spines, or other gaping orifices" [2002, 68]). But once the shock had shifted, she found herself "not repulsed, but moved to tears by the unaccountable beauty of the bodies" (69). She argues that instead of a fear of contagion from the other, we would benefit from "an ethics of relationship" (70).

It is not just a matter of having a spirit of compassion. In Shildrick's view, the monstrous bodies she discusses in her book cause unease not because they are helpless and deserving of our sympathy. Rather, our unease is prompted by the fact that the inviolability of their bodies has been breached, as in the case of Siamese twins. In a Western culture where the inviolability of the body is an indicator of self-mastery, monstrous bodies reveal all too clearly their vulnerability. The ideal of a self-contained body, secure within its own skin, unbreached, God-given as it were, marks out the disabled body, or the modified body, or the compromised, vulnerable body as its Other and as a threat and/or as repulsive. The threat is that it might contaminate. The repulsion stems from its challenge to the idealized myth of self-containment. As she comments, in our Western scientific culture, with its sovereign "I" as subject, "there is an expectation ... that our bodies are similarly under control, predictable, determinate, and above all independent in form and function" (72). The myth represses acknowledgment of our own bodily vulnerabilities, reinforcing the othering of those who fall short. So it is not about compassion so much as recognizing vulnerability—theirs *and* ours.

Shildrick does not call for the kind of empathy that characterizes contemporary television daytime talk shows or even sporting events for the differently-abled. With Paul Longmore (1997), she sees such events as yet more opportunities for normalcy to be reinforced, rather than opportunities to explore shared vulnerability. Neither is it the kind of empathy that searches for common ground and, in so doing, smooths out differences. No, it is a matter of "opening oneself—becoming vulnerable—to an encounter with irreducible strangeness," an opening to "*mutual* transformation" (Shildrick 2002, 74, emphasis added).

Informed by the work of Megan Boler (1997), Shildrick argues for a mutuality that can listen without objectifying or being paternalistic, hear without attempting to homogenize difference or assimilate the other. It involves meeting the vulnerability of the other with a radical openness to the "unpredictably strange and excessive" in a way that "renders the self vulnerable" (Shildrick 2002, 78). It maintains distinction while creating this meeting place; not swallowing the other in a faux sympathy, but recognizing that the differences between the parties are irreducible. The effect is that we become more aware of our vulnerability in terms of ontological uncertainty. In this mutuality and openness, there is understanding that "neither the one nor the other can exist apart" (131). Shildrick concludes that being prepared to acknowledge vulnerability is a "step of profound significance"

(133). It is also a step that needs to be taken by anyone who wants to shoulder ethical responsibility when interpreting texts. The relevance of this to Genesis will become clear as we turn to a discussion of trans bodies and the threat that these "monstrosities" apparently pose to religious spokespeople.

TRANS BODIES AND PRIMORDIAL ELEMENTS

Shildrick's work on the vulnerability of bodies does not deal directly with trans issues. However, she does talk about how the skin operates as a visible boundary of the self. Working with examples such as cleft palates or spina bifida, Shildrick explores how normalcy depends on bodies that are cleanly and visibly distinct—not breached, diseased, or odd. However, while transgender bodies remain discrete, bounded by skin, they are also examples of breached bodies in that they no longer have the clean lines where anatomy, sex, and gender line up in expected ways. Skin and tissue may have been excised and prosthetic additions introduced as trans people work toward the bodies they need in order to live viable lives. Transitioning (to whatever extent) morphs body lines and expected alignments:

> Hormone therapy begins this process, dramatically contravening the functioning of the gonads, refiguring the body's contours, altering tissue structure (muscle, fat, breast, genital), redistributing hair, changing skin texture in body and face. Surgery continues and radicalizes the transformation: removing sex organs … reshaping the remains and/or relocating other bodily tissues—nerves, skin, flesh—to form others. The making of these new transsexual parts (vaginoplasty, phalloplasty, mastectomy) consists in the surgical manipulation of the body's surface: the grafting, stretching, inverting, splitting, tucking, suturing of the tissues. (Prosser 1998, 66)

For some, such modifications are unnecessary and unhealthy adaptations, severing, castrating, or mutilating the otherwise healthy body. But Jay Prosser argues that such interventions should be seen more positively as offering transformative relief. "If the dominant body image pre-transition is that of being trapped within an extraneous 'other' skin, sex reassignment surgery is figured as bringing release from this skin" (82).

This "trapped in the wrong body" theme is recurrent in early trans literature. Indeed, testimony literature often indicates how the modified body feels natural and ordered while it is the birth body that (supposedly the "natural" body) can feel very alien and monstrous. Thus, when Mark

Rees (1996, 28) writes about his birth identity as female, he claims that the idea of being "destined for womanhood" was "as inconceivable as the notion of becoming a giraffe." However, we need to bear in mind that in order to qualify for any gender-reassignment surgery, candidates have to demonstrate gender dysphoria and convince a medical panel that they are alienated from their existing body. So it is small wonder that testimonies often talk of wanting to be rid of one's penis or breasts.[6]

Trans studies were placed on a new footing with Sandy Stone's "Post-transsexual Manifesto" (1991). This breaks with the earlier autobiographical literature's trajectory where the person transitions from one gender to the one newly assigned. Stone recognizes that, to some extent, those stories were necessary fictions, fulfilling the expectations and requirements of medical institutions. But the failure to "develop an effective counter-discourse" (294) left trans people passive and vulnerable to diagnostic criteria. It is better, Stone argues, to carve out a space for transsexuals to acknowledge that they "do not grow up in the same ways as 'GGs' [genuine girls], or genetic 'naturals.' Transsexuals do not possess the same history as genetic 'naturals,' and do not share common oppression prior to gender reassignment" (295). Stone's manifesto encouraged trans people to resist the urge to pass, stably and conservatively, as people who have acquired the desired gender. Better, in Stone's view, to occupy a space that is more liminal and ambiguous, a space unhinged from a rigid adherence to the sex/gender binaries. This is the situation that some trans people now occupy. As Mariette Allen (2010, 279–80) writes: "Going on hormones no longer carries the assumption that gender reassignment surgery will follow. The mixed body may be seen as beautiful and as complete as the gender-conforming body.... Fewer people feel the need to be part of 'the American Dream,' in which everyone fits in."[7]

---

6. That said, Prosser (1998, 69) argues strongly that "transsexuals continue to deploy the image of wrong embodiment because being trapped in the wrong body is simply what transsexuality feels like." He reminds us that transsexual autobiographies use the language of coming home when they go through surgery: "surgery appears as a ... restoration of the 'proper' body after the configuration of transsexual wrong embodiment" (82–83). It is not an easy homecoming, for there is no memory, no familiarity, no sense of "oh, I'm back as I should be." In reality, there are problems, and Prosser talks about how the reconstructed body can appear strange and difficult to manage. Yet he vindicates the talk of alienation from the birth body and homecoming for the chosen one.

7. For further discussion and advocacy of this position, see Bornstein 1994, 2006.

But whether we are talking about gender-ambiguous bodies or trans-sexual bodies, any deliberate disruption of the sexed and gendered body prompts theological resistance. The bodies that the Deity establishes in Gen 1:27 are taken as a divinely sanctioned template that should not be tampered with. Male and female humans are the final products of the Deity's imposition of order on the primordial elements. They are the "meant to be" inhabitants of the earth as it "should be"; designed to reproduce, the idea (and ideal) of this binary pair is a foundation stone of Western civilization, providing the "Maker's instructions" (Evangelical Alliance Policy Commission 2000, 44).

Thus it is that Gen 1:27 features strongly in the Evangelical Alliance's report that reaffirms the distinctiveness of the two sexes and the inappropriateness of crossing sex/gender boundaries. A report from the Christian Institute (2002), used as a briefing paper for voting members of the Houses of Commons and Lords in the United Kingdom, claims more strongly that it simply is not possible to change one's sex and that those who determine to live transsexually cannot live compatibly with "orthodox" Christianity. The borders are erected. The narrator of Gen 1 has provided a text that, over two millennia later, continues to keep messy elements at bay. Just as Mx. Tehom's disturbing gender-shifting qualities and mythological connotations cause such consternation that it has to be rendered utterly controllable, these reports throw an authoritative boundary around orthodoxy and attempt to push these monstrous bodies into some outside territory. Since Kristeva (1982, 4) defines abject as "what disturbs identity, system and order. What does not respect boundaries, positions, rules. The in-between, the ambiguous, the composite," it is fair to say that some religious positional statements push the trans person into the domain of the abject.

So how can the discussion above create a new way of thinking about Gen 1 and create a space for making trans lives acceptable and livable?

Trans Options for Troubling Texts

Peter Sanlon's very short book *Plastic People* (2010) provides an attempt to grapple with queer theory generally and the work of Judith Butler specifically. He is a member of the Latimer Trust Theological Work Group, who published this attempt to listen to the voices of queer theorists and consider the implications for practical Christian ministry—a commendable project. However, as much as Sanlon gives the impression of taking a considered, listening approach, he never allows this to alter his central affirmation that trans bodies run counter to God's template for humanity. His commitment to the theological notion that bodies are given to us by a creator and should not be changed inevitably undermines all the apparent listening. Sanlon hopes that his arguments enable readers to have "more confidence in holding to the conviction that a great deal of the dignity humans possess resides in the created givenness of our gendered bodies," adding that God's creation needs to be preserved, not undermined (40).

A measured tone, but ultimately a negative tone, is also apparent in the Evangelical Alliance's report (2000) on transsexuality. While regretting any "hurt caused to transsexual men and women by any unwelcoming or rejecting attitudes on the part of the church" and calling upon congregations "genuinely to welcome and accept transsexual people," the report is clear: "Authentic change from a person's given sex is not possible and an ongoing transsexual lifestyle is incompatible with God's will as revealed in Scripture and creation" (84–85). There should be no acceptance of sexually active couples where one of them is a trans person, no blessings of their relationship; and any change of a birth certificate is a "fundamentally flawed" action (87).

The Christian Institute's online briefing (2002) is even more hard-hitting. Alarmed that the United Kingdom's Gender Recognition Bill may compel churches to accept trans people who apply for employment, it defines them as those "who flagrantly reject Christian teaching that a person's biological sex is God-given." Transsexuals are "living in breath-taking defiance of their Creator" and are persisting "in sin" and "desecrating" the *imago Dei*. In its own clear construction of a firm boundary, the Christian Institute argues that "Christians" (generalized) cannot "accept a transsexual living in their assumed sex." What is required of the transsexual is "radical repentance."

Not all religious statements are so condemnatory. There is more room for maneuver in the House of Bishops' report that ponders whether it is "possible that someone's God-given sex is not identical with their physiology, and that it is therefore legitimate to allow people to change their bodies to allow this true sexual identity to be expressed" (2003, 34). Genesis 1 still features strongly, as does Oliver O'Donovan's (1982, 11) rejection of any idea that one can have a "real sex" that is other than the one given at birth; but since the report concludes with an open invitation to explore the relevance and application of scriptural texts to Christian views of transsexualism, there seems to be room for movement here.

The statements noted above do not appear to be loaded with the revulsion and loathing associated with transphobia. There is a sincere desire not to discriminate against the person, but this is hampered by the more earnest desire to uphold the template of Gen 1. However, this cannot be permitted to mask the fact that the reports are utterly permeated with genderism (defined below), which, in Darryl Hill and Brian Willoughby's view (2005), *facilitates* transphobia. For all the supposed welcoming rhetoric, there is an iron fist behind that velvet glove. In a situation where, historically, trans folk, alongside lesbian, gay, and bisexual persons, have been told that God hates them, the talk of being unacceptable, sinful, and in need of repentance continues to add to that damaging layer, particularly among LGBT people of faith.[8]

It is not just "the church" or "the synagogue" that is rejecting; religious positional statements influence congregants who may well be parents, siblings, or grandparents of trans people. Not by any means all, but some trans people will suffer rejection because of religiously informed views of their family. What is needed is a new basis for discussion, where the agency of trans people is not ruled out of court by narrow commitments to Gen 1:26–27.

Dissolving Boundaries

Let us work with the notion that the monstrous or the chaotic does not simply test boundaries or create boundaries but has the potential to dissolve them and release us from their terror. In the speech-acts of creation, the word of God does put these elements "out there" in order to separate the waters and create clearly defined substance in place of formlessness. The divine purpose seems to be entirely about creating boundaries (and in so doing, the abject) and to argue differently seems perverse. But it is better to focus not on the Deity, but on the biblical writer who creates this authoritative character. His text tells us far more about his own anxieties about the potential of the world to collapse in on itself in a deluge of waters

---

8. On the impact of religious condemnation, see Wilcox 2009. When Kate Bornstein sought help from her rabbi during transition, the rabbi cited Deut 22:5. When Bornstein tried to explain that she was not a man, the rabbi responded, "In the eyes of the Lord you are and always will be!" (Bornstein 1998, 113). Mollenkott's (2001, 81) comment on this account notes: "No empathy, no entering into the lifelong pain of a boy who had always known he was a girl, just legalistic pontificating."

that return everything to תהו ובהו. It is he who wants to hold these things at bay and needs a powerful deity to do so. In the amorphous qualities of תהו ובהו, in the gender-shifting fluidity of Mx. Tehom, the narrator faces his fears just as the cisgendered, the supposedly stably gendered person, faces the morphing qualities of the trans person that can be threatening to his or her own sense of self.

So, while transphobia can be seen as a desire to reassert clear boundaries between oneself and anything "trans," it is also a rejection of something that exists within oneself. While I do not want to homogenize the experiences of trans people with those of people who engage in different types of body modification, it is important to recognize, as Shildrick does, that the "normal" body is "always an achievement" requiring constant maintenance and/or modification to hold off the ever-present threat of disruption: extra digits are excised at birth, tongues are shortened in Down's Syndrome disease, noses are reshaped, warts removed, prosthetic limbs fitted, "healthy" diets commended, and hormone replacement therapy is prescribed. In such cases, it is the unmodified body that is seen as unnatural in need of "corrective" interventions (Shildrick 2002, 55).

Thus there may be a temptation to think of cisgendered people in terms of a stably gendered normalcy, but as the observation above indicates, body modification is actually a very broad phenomenon. Scholars like Cressida Heyes (2003, 1116) point out connections between trans body modifications and women who consider "breast implants, crash diets, or bodybuilding." Similarly, Nikki Sullivan (2006, 552) collates a number of practices within the wider occurrence of body modification: "mastectomies, penectomies, hormone treatments, tattooing, breast enhancement, implants, corsetry, rhinoplasty, scarification, branding." It is a rare human being who is so satisfied with his or her given body that one feels no need to "improve." So it is not a matter of patronizingly allowing the trans other to exist at the edges of a boundary that encircles the cisgendered; trans people challenge us to recognize that something in their desires and experiences resonates. As Shildrick (2002, 69) puts it: "The encounter with the others who define our own boundaries of normality must inevitably disturb for they are both irreducibly strange and disconcertingly familiar, both opaque and reflective. They enable us to recognize ourselves; they are our own abject."

But while there might be this resonance, based on a shared dissatisfaction with given bodies, this does not account for transphobia. Drawing on Hill's (2002) research, Hill and Willoughby (2005, 533–34) suggest that transphobia "involves the feeling of revulsion to masculine women, feminine men, cross-dressers, transgenderism and/or transsexuals."[9] Behind this, in their view, lies the ideology of *genderism*. They summarize: "genderism is the broad negative cultural ideology, transphobia is the emotional disgust and fear, and gender-bashing is the fear manifest in acts of violence" (534). The ideology of genderism, then, is what needs to be explored, and, in my view, this compels us to consider the contribution of a foundational text like Gen 1 to such an ideology. In their conclusions, Hill and Willoughby commend further research that examines "the role of traditional values such as social conformity, religious fundamentalism, conservative ideology, and moral dogmatism in the hatred of trans persons," since "a study of what trans persons symbolize for others might be a first step in further understanding anti-trans sentiments" (542).

This discussion of Gen 1 is thus partly a response to that call, demonstrating how a primary religious text can enshrine genderism and inspire in its confessional readers trans intolerance. The disturbing qualities of תהו ובהו, of Mx. Tehom, or, in my application, of the trans person, is not that they test a boundary, but that they carry the potential for dissolving boundaries. But there is a way of reading Gen 1 that does not result in kneejerk reactions against those elements. After all, תהו ובהו and Mx. Tehom play their part in the story of creation; and, as we have noted above, some argue that the invisible presence of the Deity is to be found within the primordial darkness. The stage opening of creation, for all its unsettling lack of coordinates, potentially reveals to us something of the Divine, and if we pause the scene at those opening two verses rather than rushing forward to "Let there be light" and the subsequent feats of creation, we can explore that divine presence in the qualities of formlessness and fluidity. The primordial darkness is worth staying with, lingering for a longer period in the formlessness, letting ourselves lean into that radical lack of coordinates. In this opening, the narrator has, perhaps unexpectedly, provided his readers with a connection to the *mysterium*, a liminal moment literally outside time, an opportunity for us to explore how the Divine is to be found within deep, dark, fluid presences that are not all about order and boundaries.

---

9. Their fieldwork studies, carried out among well-educated citizens of Montreal, reveal some "extremely intolerant attitudes toward gender nonconformists" (Hill and Willoughby 2005, 542), all the more surprising given this city's reputation for liberality.

To this end, we can invoke the spirit of Marcella Althaus-Reid (2003) and her criticism of theology that is heteronormative, capitalistic, colonial, and marginalizing or suppressing the voices of those it renders "other." T-theology (totalitarian, traditional theology), as she calls it, boxes God in, reducing Deity to a monotonous message delivered by monotonous messengers, makes an idol of the God Who Doesn't Change, and places limits around excessiveness. Her work encourages us to think about an inherently unstable Deity, complex and unruly, itching to be free, longing to break out of the boundaries humans have erected. The queer God is fluid, unstable, and multiple and will always be somewhat opaque, because God is both beyond us and radically here in and among us. This God unsettles and scandalizes the ramblings of T-theology, transgresses boundaries of the decent and respectable, deconstructs the center. In Althaus-Reid's view, where we might find revelations of this wonderfully unruly Deity is precisely among the people whose nonnormative sexual stories and diversities reveal to us something of "God, the Faggot; God, the Drag Queen; God, the Lesbian; God, the Heterosexual Woman who does not accept the constructions of ideal heterosexuality; God, the ambivalent, not easily classified sexuality" (2000, 95).

If we did not allow our anxieties about תהו ובהו and Mx. Tehom to dictate their banishment, perhaps we could let ourselves recognize that they tell us something about the Deity's presence within them and accept something about our own תהום, our own unbecoming. This leads us to the second way in which this chapter's discussion can help make trans lives more livable. In recognizing boundary making as an anxiety-ridden reaction to the feared threat that they pose, we see more clearly how that has led us to load the "outside" or "abject" location with negative value judgments.

CREATING SPACE FOR SHARED VULNERABILITY

Too often the trans body is cast out of the realm of the "normal" or denied agency by the paternalistic attitude and tone of religious positional statements. This has been singularly unhelpful. It renders the writers of such reports stably gendered, normal, secure, while their attempts to listen to the voices of others (even where these exist) do not put those others on an equal footing. Shildrick's (2002, 77) observation that "those on the receiving end of (limited) beneficence are never able to claim equal agency while their vulnerability remains" is pertinent, and her comments on shared vulnerability might help in the desire to create mutually respectful discussion.

For Shildrick, it is not about recognizing the other in some kind of appropriative move, neither is it a recognition of absolute difference. Rather, it is about finding "a way to inhabit that impossible point poised between assimilation and rejection where both signal the ethical bankruptcy of indifference. Responsibility lies rather in an openness to the radically, but not absolutely, unknowable other, which understands that neither the one nor the other can exist apart" (131).

Shildrick's observations prompt a serious rethinking of how biblically informed religious statements deal with the objects (abjects) of their discourse. It is not appropriate for such statements to be written about trans people without having a mutual conversation with those people. This is not just about requesting that some representative trans voices make a contribution to a cisgendered panel. It is more than an attempt to listen to the other and then deliberating. It is about radical openness to *shared* vulnerability. When Shildrick is confronted with that *Still Life* exhibition and recovers from the shock of it, she shifts from fear of contagion and opens herself to the encounter with "irreducible strangeness" and in so doing is open to "*mutual* transformation" (74). It is that readiness to acknowledge vulnerability that is the "step of profound significance" (133). What is called for from religious spokespersons, committees, panels, and indeed the biblical and theological scholars whose work informs those groups is humility and readiness to accept their *own* transformation in the encounter. As we have seen, the terminology of existing reports is a long way from this. In a telling comment, Shildrick observes, "It is only those who have no wish to cede the authority and power that they hold … who need fear the monsters" (133). That is what this is ultimately about: the willingness to unshed power, authority, and the conviction that one is undeniably right.

What stands in the way of this is the Bible and the belief that the creation stories provide a deity's template for two, and only two, sexes; that the order and beneficence of creation lies in banishing the confusions and disorientations of תהו ובהו and תהום. Is it possible to work through this apparent immovable hurdle for those who wish to uphold an authoritative significance for Scripture? There are a number of options.

As argued above, תהו ובהו and תהום can be seen as containers of invisible divine presence. They are not elements that are outside that orbit. Indeed, the Bible knows a quite playful side of the Deity's relationship with sea monsters. In Job 41, the Deity recalls all the monstrous features of Behemoth and Leviathan. Behemoth has ribs like iron bars and is powerfully built, most ferocious, a foe to anyone who desires his capture. Leviathan is a beast whose sneeze makes the sunlight sparkle like lightning, who ejects fire and smoke from its mouth and nostrils, who reduces humans to terror. Yet the Deity can take this beast for a gambol in the sea and declare that he is also the creator of Behemoth. The monstrous is part of creation, not lurking at its boundaries but fully within. Sitting down with Behemoth and Leviathan, or with Mx. Tehom, might take some nerve; but it is that quiet sitting alongside, opening oneself to their irreducibly strange presence, and letting them open to ours that might engender mutuality.

We can heed the calls of Justin Tanis (2000) and Victoria Kolakowski (1997b) for compassionate hermeneutics and the readiness to imagine a more diverse world. Imagine, says Tanis, people of faith declaring their happy realization that people come in all shapes and sizes, including genders and sexualities. Envisage their surprise as they encounter "those who see themselves as no gender, those who cross genders, transgender, monogamous, polygamous, nonmonogamous, people with many ways of loving, people who are celibate, old, young, ageless," and conclude that God loves wondrous variety and is "even greater than we ever dreamed" (Tanis 2000, 52).

If possible, we can try to dissociate the rhetoric, fears, and anxieties of a human narrator from the Deity that the narrator proposes to define. This would recognize that biblical texts, unfortunately, have historically sanctioned all manner of unjustified violence, for which the church has subsequently apologized.

Conclusion

Reading backwards has commonality with reading askance, reading against the grain, reading from left to right. What all these things have in common is challenge and justice. Genesis 1 is a text that is significantly "alive." Reading "with" the text encourages us to validate a process of becoming that marks the abject at the same time. Reading backwards allows us to re-collect what has been lost or marginalized and to see the mechanics of a text that creates an atmosphere in which heteronormativity can live and breathe, but where gender/sex transgression is banished to the abject. We have an ethical responsibility to challenge collusion with texts that diminish the lives of people. If we are not to consign Gen 1 to the waste bin, then ways of working with the text have to be found. It has been my unexpected delight to find, in the process of reading backwards, a way of finding the divine right at the heart of the Other.

3

Modeling the Transgender Gaze:
Performances of Masculinities in 2 Kings 9–10

Deryn Guest

I wanted to be Troy Tempest. Yes, there were other appealing television characters to inhabit for street play in the 1960s: Virgil Tracey, Captain Scarlet, the Virginian, Tarzan; but Troy Tempest was the identity of choice. And I played the part well; organizing my clothing, tone of voice, hair, and mannerisms to fit the character. Of course, I always got to kiss the girl who was occupying the role of Atlanta or Marina. All this without ever reading a page of Leslie Feinberg.[1] The queer child is a material fact; perhaps puzzled by sex and gender norms but having remarkably resilient fluidity for working out preferred gender categories (though becoming troubled when the body, during puberty, belies that choice). Butch lesbian and trans literature is littered with autobiographical narratives and images of cross-gender identification and queer childhoods. There is hardly any material, however, on how children make their own queer negotiations with biblical characters, despite the fact that young readers are adept at making literature speak to their desires.[2] If I could be Troy Tempest in the street, what parts could I occupy within the pages of a Bible? What happens when a person assigned "female" at birth has FTM[3] leanings and uses them to inhabit that supposedly "male" space? How does this queer the text?

---

1. Leslie Feinberg is known for creating an activist movement around transgender. *Stone Butch Blues* (1993) was later formative for my own identity.

2. See Jessica Kander (2011) for a discussion of how queer subtexts can be read in children's and youth literature, and Alison Hennegan's (1988) essay on making straight literature speak to her own desires.

3. FTM (some prefer lower case) abbreviates female-toward-male or female-to-

In our evangelical household, the hefty *Children's Bible in Colour* (1964; hereafter *CBIC*) was a primary text. Its representations of characters and events viscerally grabbed a child's imagination. The illustrations, executed by the Fabbri Studios under the direction of Sandro Nardini and Aldo Torchio, provide flesh, color, movement, and background imagery for stories heard only aurally (but repeatedly) at Sunday school. I did less reading of this tome and more copying out and coloring in of the pictures. The images of masculinity found therein were vivid and attractive: Gideon, with his designer stubble, strong chin, head scarf manfully arranged, sending his soldiers forth into battle. The scantily clad, muscle-honed, luxuriantly haired Samson battling with lions was another favorite, particularly the full-page depiction of the chained, blind, and doomed hero bringing down the Philistine temple. Jacob has none of the rather effeminate features that appear in the biblical text; here he appears as a Greek Adonis with short wiry hair, toned muscles, strong calves, and good cheekbones (though do note the homoerotic depiction of him lying asleep, robe falling away from his torso, as he dreams of the angelic escalator).

But the illustration I returned to regularly was of Jehu: another muscularly defined Adonis, appealingly adorned in a bright blue loincloth, bearing a quiver that color-coordinated with his red and gold chariot. His taut left arm holds a magnificent bow as he aims an arrow directly at King Joram. While my mother had little inkling of the gender alignments that were being made as I sketched out favorite images and inhabited them, she had unwittingly handed me a style guide for male performativity. I could ease myself into these stories with a gender fluidity that perhaps only a child can do so effortlessly. As unlikely as it seems, an illustrated Bible was probably my first encounter with subverting gender alignments, providing a way of occupying the gender that instinctively felt right. It is that early memory of Jehu's image that prompts my choice of text to explore how

---

male. This is not a term reserved solely for transitioning persons but can be used "as a general rubric for any number of potential life trajectories, not just the transsexual ones" (Hale 1998, 341 n. 1). FTM and its variations (F_2M, F_tM, F-t-M) are rejected by those who prefer MTM (male to male) since they never felt themselves to be women in the first place. Serano rejects turning these abbreviations into nouns since the people concerned may not identify as a "female-to-male" but as man. Better to use them adjectivally so that it does not "disregard the profoundly felt gender identity of the transsexual in question" nor "the very real experiences that trans person has had being treated as a member of the sex that they have transitioned to" (2007, 30).

a transgender gaze might operate, as I return to Jehu to see what a more theoretically astute, adult Deryn can do with him.

In the discussion that follows, I do not provide a detailed exegesis of 2 Kgs 9–10, nor do I make any assumptions about the historicity of events described in the narrative. Rather, I use this narrative as a case study for exploring what happens when one engages with a biblical text with a transgender gaze at the forefront of the reading experience in order to formulate a heuristic model of transgender engagement. En route, I consider what differentiates a butch lesbian reading of a text from a trans reading and who owns the transgender gaze. I demonstrate the need for theory-rich awareness and "trans literacy" among biblical scholars in order to negotiate successfully this complex terrain. With a clear nod to Viviane Namaste's (2009) work, I call for a practical understanding of how this engagement must be held accountable for the effects it generates.

MODELING THE TRANSGENDER GAZE

Transgender engagement with biblical texts could follow several avenues of interest. It could involve historical and cultural studies by looking at instances of transgender within the ancient Near East generally and more specifically within ancient Israel.[4] It could work with germane themes such as transformation, liminality, crossings, displacement, gender variance, hybridity, and borderlands. It could also involve work on biblical characters that appear to have trans significance or resonance, such as Joseph or the eunuch.[5] However, these areas are not concerned directly with what the transgender gaze can produce or how it might operate; and, without considering this, all the above ideas run the risk of making transgender an object of scrutiny rather than giving it hermeneutic agency.

---

4. Hoffner (1966) and Nissinen (1998), for example, draw attention to the Galli, the eunuch priests of Cybele, the bearded Ishtar credited with the ability to transform a man into a woman, and Anat's male performativity. Hoffner (1966, 333) poses the intriguing question of why ancient men/women might desire to "wear the attire or symbols of the opposite sex" and posits some answers, though, ultimately, he is unable to provide a convincing rationale for the command of Deut 22:5. More work on why a Deuteronomic law prohibits the accoutrements of masculinity appearing on a woman and vice versa is needed, particularly in the light of emerging trans studies within the academy.

5. On Joseph, see Carden 2006; and for discussions on eunuchs, see Kolakowski 1997a, 2000; Kuefler 2001; Stanley 2006; K. Stone 2006; West 2006.

When queer readings emerged, they disrupted the objectification of lesbian, gay, bisexual, or transgender categories and, instead, put heteronormativity under the critical spotlight. So, while there may well be some political gains to be made by focusing on texts that have been used to resist acceptance of transsexuality, such as Deut 22:5, here I examine what happens to a text with no apparent trans significance when interpreted from a trans perspective.

There is hardly anything written on how such a gaze can interrogate literature, but Judith Halberstam's (2001) analysis of the film *Boys Don't Cry* offers a starting point. This film is based on the life of the twenty-one-year-old Brandon, who, along with two friends, was murdered in 1993. Described by C. Jacob Hale (1998, 311) as "a gender-ambiguous young person who had lived for several years in a butch/ftm border zone," Brandon's murder appears to be closely linked with his gender presentation, though detailed knowledge of how Brandon self-identified is sketchy.[6]

In the film, a scene is reproduced where Brandon's male friends suspect that he is female-bodied and subject him to a brutal examination. While this is happening to Brandon on the floor, the film depicts a fully clothed Brandon looking on from the doorway, and it is the gaze of this second Brandon that Halberstam identifies with the transgender gaze.

First, for Halberstam, the transgender gaze is thus integrally connected to the trans persons themselves and has agency (though it should be noted that Brandon was obviously not alive when the film was made and his viewpoint is being forged by the director, Kimberly Peirce, and the actress, Hilary Swank, entering empathetically into his world). As Brandon looks out on what is happening to him, the transgender gaze has an agency that is simultaneously being removed forcibly from the Brandon who is being

---

6. The birth name of this individual was Teena Renae Brandon, though various names were used during his lifetime, including Brandon Teena, Charles Brandon, Billy Brandon, and Brandon Brayman. I use "Brandon" in my discussion. However, I appreciate Hale's (1998, 314) observation that insisting on a certain variant of name and gender pronoun can produce "a representation of someone more solidly grounded in gendered social ontology than the subject (recon)figured by that name actually might have been." Hale prefers to refer to "him" in quotation marks, thereby acknowledging our lack of certain knowledge, a practice I have not continued, because the quotation marks risk presenting Brandon as freakish and undermine any male identity that Brandon may have wished to preserve. Discussion of Brandon's life demonstrates the limits of our vocabulary, which grammatically does not encourage imagining beyond the very limited gender binary of his/her and the neuter "it."

pinned to the floor. But the Brandon who is watching from the doorway owns his own truth and alternative reality. The watching Brandon, witnessing himself being attacked, is the one who knows himself to be male no matter what his physiology might be.

Second, however, while this transgender gaze has the agency of ownership, it is also fragile. It has to secure itself despite the radical insecurities that come from knowing that its alternative knowledge can be brutally and violently rejected by others.

Third, it needs acknowledgment and validation from allies. In the case of *Boys Don't Cry*, this comes from Lana. In a preceding scene, where the men threaten to strip Brandon, Lana says she will do the regulatory check. But, alone with Brandon, she tells him not to continue unbuckling his trousers, for she knows he is a boy. As Halberstam comments (2001, 296), "The clothed Brandon is the Brandon rescued by Lana's refusal to look, the Brandon who survives his own rape and murder." The transgender gaze is thus one that knows itself despite the supposed knowledge of those who rely on literal physiology to ascertain sex and gender but still need the validation that can come from another. Halberstam again: "Brandon can be Brandon because Lana is willing to see him as he sees himself (clothed, male, vulnerable, lacking, strong, passionate), and to avert her gaze when his manhood is in question" (296). Halberstam is more equivocal about whether the director also acts as validator since, ultimately, the film cannot hold the transgender gaze. This implies that the role of validator is important but, perhaps, difficult to sustain in a world that is relentlessly heteronormative.

Fourth, the transgender gaze problematizes notions of stable sex and gender, because it locates a male gaze in a body not sexed as male. The film holds in tension Brandon's maleness, which in his head and Lana's head is real, and the contrary male gaze of other characters whose knowledge "resides in the literal" (Halberstam 2001, 295). For them, a person is male only if their body testifies accordingly. The maleness that Brandon lives out is unhinged from the sexed body, more like a cultural space that he occupies. From this position, Brandon is able to operate a male gaze that can be critical of dominant masculinities, as seen, for example, in the care he apparently took with his real-life girlfriends.[7] Indeed, this gaze has the

---

7. Donna Minkowitz's article unfortunately uses female pronouns throughout, thereby reconstituting Brandon as a woman. Nevertheless, her acknowledgment of how Brandon did masculinity in a girl-pleasing way is worth noting: "However they

ability to shift narrative paradigms. Halberstam notes how Brandon occupies "the position in the romance which is usually allotted to the male hero and the male gaze"; and whereas the female body can be indicative of lack or powerlessness, here it is Brandon who "represents the general condition of incompleteness, crisis and lack, and it is Lana who represents the fantasy of wholeness, knowledge and pleasure" (296).

To summarize, what we learn from Halberstam's analysis is that the transgender gaze bears certain hallmarks. It holds up an alternative vision for the reader, one fragile yet resilient, one that needs the confirmation of the others against the prevailing norms that would discount it, one where expectations of sex and gender are criticized or destabilized and narrative paradigms are shifted. It is a gaze that fights against abjection and erasure for the survival of its different imagining, and it is a gaze embodied in the transgendered person.

In the next section, I keep these points in mind as I analyze what happens when a transgender gaze is applied to the story of Jehu. This, of course, is a different project from that of Halberstam. For Halberstam, the gaze emerges from a filmic presentation with overt transgender themes. It is already "within" the film looking out. In this paper, the transgender gaze derives from the writer, who is located "outside" the text, looking in. This inevitably produces different emphases and observations; but as we shall see, there are strong commonalities between the two approaches, and my proposed heuristic model for transgender interpretation includes the following elements, each of which is unpacked in detail below:

1. It locates the transgender gaze in trans experience.
2. It exposes the constructedness of gender (noting how sex/gender stability is maintained and how disruptions to it are suppressed).

---

classify Brandon, everybody wants her. From photos of the wonder-boychik playing pool, kissing babes, and lifting a straight male neighbor high up in the air to impress party goers at her and Gina's engagement party, Brandon looks to be the cutest butch item in history—not just good-looking, but arrogant, audacious, cocky—everything they, and I, look for in lovers. Her bereaved girlfriends are leery of describing sexual details, but it's glaringly clear Brandon was the precise opposite of a 'do me' feminist.... You could call Brandon a top, but I'm not sure that word fully captures her enormous desire to give other people pleasure" (1994, 27).

3. It confronts heteronormativity with alternative visions of gender that may be fragile but are resilient and capable of shifting paradigms of existing thought.
4. It requires political and religious engagement, challenging the (negative) effects of biblical interpretation for trans people.

Owning the Transgender Gaze

My decision to lean into an FTM position for the purpose of writing this chapter immediately sets a number of alarm bells ringing. Who can own or occupy the transgender gaze? How does this differ from a transsexual gaze or a butch lesbian gaze? What definitions inform this discussion?

In a paper originally published in 1992, Leslie Feinberg (2006, 205) initiated an activist approach for those who defied the "'man'-made boundaries of gender." Noting that such defiance had already provoked labeling by others, such as "he-shes" (206), Feinberg advocated terminology that could *self*-define a community of like-minded gender resisters who, though diverse, could form a movement. *Transgender* subsequently emerged as a

> "pangender" umbrella term for an imagined community encompassing transsexuals, drag queens and butches, hermaphrodites, cross-dressers, masculine women, effeminate men, sissies, tomboys, and anybody else willing to be interpolated by the term, who felt compelled to answer the call to mobilization. (Stryker 2006, 4)

Since then, *transgender* has often been used as an umbrella term into which a range of people can fit. A. Finn Enke (2012, 4) thus notes how transgender might include "FTM, MTF, gender queer, trans woman, trans man, butch queen, fem queen, tranny, transy, drag king, bi-gender, pangender, femme, butch, stud, two spirit, people with intersex conditions, androgynous, gender-fluid, gender euphoric, third gender, *and* man and woman." Definitions in other sources inevitably add or omit terms, but the general sense of *transgender* as incorporating an assortment of lived experiences is clear.[8]

---

8. For further definitions of transgender, see Cromwell 1999, 26; Sullivan 2003, 112; Whittle 2006, xi. Cromwell (1999, 22) also introduces the term *transgenderismt,*

My use of *transgender* follows these broad inclusions. My personal position is close to that of Jack Halberstam (2012), who would like top surgery but at the time of writing does not envisage taking hormones, is not formally transitioned, and varies between male and female pronouns in order to own a gender ambiguity. I have much in common with trans men: an alignment with the styling of "the masculine" and very early knowledge that I exited the "woman" category or that I was never in it to begin with. But those markers can also be indicative of the butch lesbian.

Butchness can be understood in terms of being not-woman; so Amber Hollibaugh and Cherríe Moraga (1983, 394): "To be butch, to me, is not to be a woman." Gayle Rubin (1992, 467) sees butchness as "the lesbian vernacular term for women who are more comfortable with masculine gender codes, styles, or identities than with feminine ones." Sherrie Innes and Michele Lloyd (1996, 27) argue that masculinity is the "chief identifying trait of the butch," that is, "not sexual desire and choice of sexual object." Hale observes,

> some butches might have richer, more solid male or masculine self-identifications that do some ftms. Consequently, drawing a distinction between butches and ftms in terms of masculine subjectivity threatens to elide both some ftms' self-identifications and some butches' self-identifications relative to the categories "man," "male," and "masculine." (1998, 322)

Yet for others, butch sits alongside a female identity. Drawing on discussion conference panels and two soirée discussions on androgyny and butch/femme, JoAnne Loulan (1990, 134) cites the following view on how to define butch: "It's not an imitation of a man, I've been with men, but that wasn't my experience. Women are present. A strong silent woman is still there and present for you." Kirsten Hill (cited in Apner, 1998, 107) is rather more emphatic: "butches push the limits and explore the boundaries of gender identity not because they try to be men, but because they express and display their masculinity *while remaining women*. Butch, then, is a distinctly feminine appropriation of the masculine" (emphasis added).

---

for those who "neither want nor desire sex reassignment surgery" but who "live the majority of their lives in a gender that opposes their biological sex. They may or may not identify as men or women, and they may identify as either/or, neither/nor, or both and."

As Emily Apter (1998, 107) comments, "Rather than see butch masculine-identification as an erasure of the feminine … Hill presents it as a strategy for resignifying femininity. The butch feminine is conceived of as that which alters and enlarges the feminine Symbolic."

So there is no one-size-fits-all definition of butch lesbian; each individual will locate herself uniquely on the gender spectrum—some far more within the category of the masculine and without any wish to resignify femininity; and here, arguably, the territory between butch lesbian and FTM gets sharply divided. But FTM identities are not clear-cut either. Hale (1998, 321) notes, "Masculine subjectivity cannot be simply reduced to self-identification as a man, for not all ftms self-identify as men in any simple, nonproblematic way." Hale goes on to mention alternatives such as those who see their transsexual identity as a completely different gender, those who consider themselves hybrid genders, and those who identify in third gender terms. Jason Cromwell (1999, 27) talks of the "gray areas between trans- and butch identities." Border wars, in his view, derive "from places of misunderstanding; neither side clearly understands the other's perspective. From some FTM/transmen perspectives, butches are transsexuals in denial; from some butches' perspectives, FTM/transmen are misguided lesbians" (28). Controversy and conflict also derive from the desire to erect boundaries around categories, especially when one has disowned a previous identity category in favor of another or when one group wants to retain the "femaleness" of lesbian identities despite some stone butches saying clearly that they do not identify as women.[9] Amid these debates and contestations are the bodies of the border zone dwellers: those who "are trying to live in the nearly unspeakable spaces created by the overlapping margins of distinct categories" (Hale 1998, 319).

Within this debate, I find myself an unhappy straddler: I have self-tagged as butch lesbian in most of my writing to date, but I have FTM affinity and regularly ponder surgery and transitioning. It is an uncomfortable place to be; and, at the time of writing, I use *transgender* in its encompassing capacity and have empathy with Hale's view that "Borders between gender categories … are zones of overlap, not lines" (323).

As for the term *transsexual*, I follow convention in reserving this for those who are at some point on a surgical sex-reassignment journey, while

---

9. For further discussion of the "border wars," see Halberstam 1998, 141–73.

acknowledging that the divide is not so simplistic as it can seem. I favor making the distinction in order to recognize the particularities of transsexual experiences and oppressions. Yet a distinction is unhelpful if it reifies noncomplex notions of transsexuality, isolates transsexuals, or gives the impression that they should be left to form their own activist community. It is even more unhelpful when the distinction between transgender and transsexual falls foul of a spurious value judgment wherein transgender is valued as a queer, progressive, political statement while transsexuality becomes the marker of easily assimilated, binary-reinforcing living.[10] Sandy Stone's "Posttranssexual Manifesto" (1991), which called upon transsexuals to resist disappearing into heteronormative society after transition, inevitably invoked a divide between those whose strong desire was to do just that and those who took up the alternative vision of the manifesto. Stone had noted that gender reassignment discourses consigned transsexuals to invisibility by fading them into "the 'normal' population as soon as possible" but argued that it was "difficult to generate a counterdiscourse if one is programmed to disappear" (295). Adopting a posttranssexual identity, which would not seek to pass as convincingly "male" or "female" but requires to be read as a different occupancy of gender, could, arguably, subvert the sex binary. Posttranssexual activist Kate Bornstein (1994) has accordingly challenged the view that one has to occupy fully a gender category and hopes the transgender revolution will create a very different future world where the limited categories of male/female are transformed. Bornstein's position chimes resonantly with Mariette Allen's (2010, 279) claim that times have changed: "Going on hormones no longer carries the assumption that gender reassignment surgery will follow. The mixed body may be seen as beautiful and as complete as the gender-conforming body."

It is easy to see how the "woodworking" person's gendernaut credentials can get devalued by these developments and how relatively easy it is for some feminists to continue denouncing transsexuals as dupes of gender.[11] This divide, however, is too easily made, and participants in the

---

10. The argument can also work the other way: transsexuality becomes "representative of an 'authentic' experience" against which "the transgenderist is positioned as an almost frivolous postmodern player" (Hines 2006, 51).

11. Historically, this was the position taken by Janice Raymond (1979), Mary Daly (1978), Germaine Greer (1999), and Sheila Jeffreys (2003), who criticized (MTF) transsexuality as a damaging fantasy that could never match experiential knowledge

debate need to hear the voices of transsexuals and the importance of bodily transition for some people. Jay Prosser (1998, 84), for example, reminds contemporary theorists of the importance of the materiality of the body, particularly how one mediates a sense of self through the skin. To this end, immersion in the preferred gender body is of vital importance. However, Prosser is profoundly aware that this immersion is complex. Surgery does not mean one can slide into an alternative gender and find oneself finally and fully at home. The reassigned person does not inherently know how to handle the new, strange body, and there is no easy assimilation. This awareness is raised more emphatically by Judith Halberstam (1998, 164), who observes that "some bodies are never at home, some bodies cannot simply cross from A to B, some bodies recognize and live with the inherent instability of identity."

However, there is another reason why "woodworking" into society and having one's chosen gender successfully recognized happens—and this concerns survival. If one is to be safe in a reassigned body, some measure of assimilation may well be necessary. The anxiety provoked by Brandon's gender ambiguity ended in his murder, and for MTF people, this danger seems even more likely (see Namaste 2000). Accordingly, a convincing display of femininity is important for living safely on the streets. But survival also has to be achieved on a more mundane, day-to-day basis. Patricia Gagné and Richard Tewksbury's (1998) research documents how gender is always accomplished in interaction with others. When those others are faced with a person who does not fit into binary categories, there is unease. Recognition and acceptance thus comes at the cost of

---

that comes from being born as, and positioned as, "woman" within a patriarchal society. No man, however empathetic, or however surgically reassigned, could fully appreciate what it is to have had that female history. Any such fantasy was considered damaging because (1) it brought impostors into "woman space"; (2) the conservative ways in which some MTFs were embodying femininity threatened to undo the political work feminists were doing to expand and redefine gender; and (3) the sense of being, innately, in the wrong body, was out of tune with social constructionist understandings of gender. So, in this strand of feminist thought, only women-born-women could occupy the female subject position, and transsexuals were, at best, unwanted plastic penetrators of women-space who did not just hold up progress but reversed it. For more recent discussions along these lines see Golden 2000; Hausman 2001; and Burkett 2015. For a critical discussion of such views, see Heyes 2003; and for a recent challenge to the opposition of a subversive transgender political position versus the supposed conservative transsexual, see Lane 2009.

hiding the trans elements of oneself, occupying the other gender entirely, because the wider societal desire for conformity cannot cope with overt ambiguity. This does not mean that the initial breaking of the organic connection between sex and gender has not happened. If we pause at the transitional phase, we see how the gender binary fails, in that the transitioning process counters any "'natural' outgrowth of biological sex" (86). We should not lose that insight. Transitioning *is* subversive of normative assumptions. But, in order to avoid the unease of others and concomitant danger, the pressures are "to transform completely and convincingly from social manhood to womanhood" (86). The problem is not with the transsexual; the problem is with the limitations of cultural norms, employers, and personal relations, which compel transsexuals to comply with *their* needs. Gagné and Tewksbury's research revealed an array of stories where even "the most understanding employers expected full-time immediate transformation.... Either the individual was fired or pressured to quit, or she was pressured to transform quickly and convincingly" (92).

So, the road to transsexuality *does* subvert supposed coherence between sex and gender. It disturbs, it unhinges expectations, and it prompts violence. But once the chosen gender is inhabited, do we lose that subversion, because the person occupying it is pressured to demonstrate that their sex and gender are congruent? No. The lived femininity (or masculinity) is a different femininity.

The above discussion explains why my emphasis on a transgender gaze in this chapter does not reflect any devaluation of transsexuality, nor does the distinction between the transsexual and transgender imply the political superiority of one term over the other. I choose *transgender*, because I have not embarked on any hormonal or surgical changes. I fit best within the broad category of transgender, and this is the place from which I can write. I do not wish to infer transsexuality as a "limit case" that forms the boundary around my transgender reading position and enables readers to dismiss transsexuality from view.[12] I welcome transsexual engagement with biblical texts; I simply do not presume that I am equipped to write them.

The ownership of the gaze, then, lies with those who identify within an inclusive transgender space. Their experiences of living within hetero-

---

12. Hale (1998, 317) warns of how transsexuality can act as a limit case, a boundary, that once "duly noted and tucked safely out of sight" can be dropped from further discussion.

normativity provide subjugated knowledges that inform trans readings of texts. As Cromwell (1999, 7) replied, when asked how far his lived experience as a trans man gave him particular insights: "I know what kinds of questions to ask, I recognize the talk we use and what it means within particular contexts; and, as an insider, I understand what it means to be a female-bodied transperson." His "trans-tinted" glasses facilitate a viewing position that is different from the cisgendered person: "my perspective allows me to see and interpret things in a way that individuals who are not transpeople do not or would not" (7). Notwithstanding, he knows that his reality is specific only to him and that he cannot speak for the many. I concur. Individuals will have different approaches, and their criticisms of the model I am proposing will be welcome. But this does not detract from my view that the trans gaze in biblical studies is owned by those whose in-house knowledge and experiences provide the trigger for critical observation and insights.

Making Visible the Construction of Gender

Children with transgender leanings are acutely alert to how the masculine is performed. They observe closely the gestures and gait of masculinity, its clothing styles, its linguistics and tone. The *CBIC*'s illustration of Jehu provides its distinctive visual portrayal of performed masculinity. It is muscular, white, tanned, rugged, and skilled (he remains balanced in a racing chariot despite both hands being occupied with bow and arrow). Jehu embodies a masculinity that seems heroic, courageous, active, and attractive.

Those qualities, to some extent, cohere with the text. The Jehu narrative resounds with imperatives, rapid action, underdog boldness, and competitiveness. However, when these are mentioned in existing studies, it is due to an interest in *character*. Treated as character traits, they are discussed alongside some less appealing qualities, such as brutality, cold ruthlessness, bloodthirstiness. Yet there is no coverage on how such qualities are linked to his performance of masculinity. The transgender gaze is alert precisely to this performativity, and one of its primary strengths is the ability to unpack masculinity's most successful characteristic: its ability to naturalize itself. Jehu's masculinity can no longer be a feature of the text that can "function without challenge or question" (Reeser 2010, 7) but needs to be mapped. Marking masculinity is one of the best strategies for problematizing it, and in the discussion below, I expose six areas where Jehu is doing "masculinity."

Jehu: The Man's Man

Jehu is introduced, unusually, with a double male heritage. His father and grandfather are mentioned in 2 Kgs 9:2, again at 9:14, with a further single reference to Nimshi at 9:20.[13] There are no details of female relatives. We are also informed that he will be found among his brothers, subsequently defined as שרי החיל, his fellow officers in the army. Walter Brueggemann (2000, 383) describes the atmosphere well when he talks about Jehu being with "his fellow officers at the officers club." I concur with Lissa Wray Beal that his presence among these brothers implies congeniality and gruff familiarity—as seen in the easy camaraderie of his men calling him a liar and pressing him to tell them what really happened in the inner room. It is a masculinity at ease with itself and with other men, even if, as Wray Beal goes on to point out, Jehu is cagey in response: he "plays his cards close to his chest" until he has ascertained what these men make of the anointing (2007, 70). Male companionship continues to accompany and surround Jehu as the story proceeds—Bidkar, Jehonadab, and the men who suddenly fall in with his orders (the riders, the eunuchs). Whether the last group's switch of allegiance is due to Jehu's charisma or because they fear his reprisals is unclear. What is abundantly clear, however, is that Jehu is a man who needs no woman and is not in any way female-identified. The only woman mentioned in Jehu's narrative is Jezebel, whose "harlotries and sorceries" merit her execution. His aversion to Jezebel is such that he cannot utter her name or speak with her. When she addresses him from the palace window, he completely ignores her taunt and, instead, questions her eunuchs. Whose side are they on? When instructing his attendants to bury her, still her name does not pass his lips; she is the "accursed woman." Rather than being described as a queen mother or queen consort in her own right, he acknowledges her only as the "daughter of a king." Phyllis Trible (1995, 177), who notes this flinching from the feminine, writes: "Male bonding, even between enemies, motivates Jehu. Jezebel as queen he discounts." Jehu thus models a form of masculinity noted more widely: one that is female/feminine-avoidant.[14]

---

13. Some, such as Hens-Piazza (2006, 287), suggest that Nimshi is a clan name but this would still locate Jehu in the world of male ancestry.

14. This feature of masculinity is observed by Strathern 1988; Gilmore 1990, 1996; Chapman 2004; Clines 1995; and Haddox 2010. Jehu's female-avoidant, arguably misogynist masculinity is not new to biblical interpreters. It has been recognized

This is not a character trait so much as a defining feature of masculinity. It is presented as entirely normal and not worthy of any specific comment by the biblical writer or subsequent commentators. But it deserves attention, because it reinforces and successfully ring-fences the domain of masculinity, with femininity inevitably set up as its counter-category, on which masculinity actually depends for definition. Jehu is masculine, because he is not feminine: a man's man with no mention of female dependence.

Jehu's Accoutred Masculinity

Masculinity is signified by the accoutrements that one adopts (see Hoffner 1966), and Jehu is equipped with three key signifiers of masculinity: the bow, the arrow, and the chariot. Indeed, his story is remarkable for the "large amount of vocabulary that associates Jehu with chariots, horses, riding, and other military accoutrements and actions" (White 1997, 30). The narrator thus presents again a feminine-avoidant form of masculinity, for no one would have associated Jehu with distaff and spindle: this is a man carefully surrounded with the correct accessories. When Deut 22:5 commands that no "thing" that belongs to a גבר should appear on a woman, we see the construction of gender at work; and, as Athalya Brenner (1997) suggests, male-only dress and equipment indicate attempts to safeguard male autonomy and social supremacy. Jehu is thus not only a man's man, but he is cast with all the (restricted) symbols that mark out masculinity.

Jehu's Violent Ruthlessness

Our initial meeting with Jehu takes place at Ramoth-gilead, a place of refuge for homicides who had killed unintentionally. No doubt it was also a strategic army base, but knowing the Hebrew writer's enjoyment of

---

as a problem by feminist scholars for some time. To read with the grain of the text, to adopt its androcentric perspective, is always to read against women's interests. What is distinctive about the transgender approach is the conflict it provokes for the exegete whose MTF position coexists with an allegiance to feminist politics. The FTM reader cannot take up the banner of feminism uncritically, because certain strands of feminism have, historically, been hostile and damaging to trans people. The trans reader cannot *unequivocally* be in the feminist camp; it demands a negotiation of feminism, a trans-nuanced feminism—but, I would argue, not a compromised one.

meaningful place names, one might legitimately ask what connotations are implied by having Jehu situated in a place designated for people who are in trouble for "accidental" killing. Certainly, the death toll in this narrative is striking, moving swiftly from named single figures (Joram, Ahaziah, and Jezebel) to anonymous groups: "seventy sons" of Ahab;[15] forty-two kinsmen of Ahaziah; the officials, priests, and intimates of Ahab's retinue in Samaria; and a massacre of Baal worshipers.[16] One of his most ruthless acts is the possible trampling of Jezebel's body. While the Masoretic Text has the singular verb, with Jehu being the most obvious subject, driving his chariot over her,[17] English translations tend to go with the Septuagint, Syriac, and targum plural, so that it is the horses that do the trampling. From royal assassination to bloodbath, Jehu's masculinity is intrinsically connected to killing (Joram) and ensuring that other men (and animals) kill upon his order.

There is a difference between identifying such killing in terms of a character trait, for example, describing Jehu as bloodthirsty (Ellul 1972, 99) and seeing killing as an aspect of masculine performativity. Masculinity solidifies into hegemonic norms when behaviors and attitudes get reinscribed repeatedly and, in so doing, become naturalized. The capacity for violence can thus become a congealed, sedimentary layer in what it means to be masculine. If this goes unremarked, we reinforce, rather than problematize, a connection between masculinity and killing. Harold Washington has already demonstrated how Deuteronomic war laws create a discourse of male power. They "valorize violent acts, construe them as essential to male agency, and define licit conditions for their exercise" (1997, 344). Deuteronomic narratives contribute to the same discourse of male power when major characters like Jehu embark upon untempered killings. Washington has convincingly demonstrated how "conventional historical criticism has often transparently reinscribed these gender constructions" (332).

---

15. Seventy is a typological number indicative of "all possible claimants to the throne" (Cogan and Tadmor 1988, 113).

16. On the shift from named victims to the murder of whole groups without any remembrance of individual names, see García-Treto 1992, 166.

17. So Wray Beal (2007, 94), with Cogan and Tadmor also arguing that the "MT singular with Jehu as subject is the more striking reading and adds to the characterization of the protagonist" (1988, 112).

Jehu's actions are so extraordinary that commentators have often pulled themselves out of the narrative in order to pass an ethical comment or to question how far the Deuteronomist could be endorsing such violence.[18] On the other hand, when Jehu's actions are understood as a by-product of a Yahwist reform movement, the connection between gender and violence elides into a discussion of Jehu's "zeal." For some (G. Jones 1984, 450; Leithart 2006, 223), Jehu's zeal is positively endorsed by the Deuteronomist. But in these discussions, the connection between masculinity and violence goes unremarked. We need to note how the killings orchestrated by Jehu reinscribe the masculine as the gender that kills and normalizes it, so that Jehu merely stands in a long biblical tradition of men-killing-men, reinforcing the norm.[19] When the killing is excessive, commentators are uneasy and the killer's motives come under scrutiny but not, it seems, the larger connection between masculinity, male power, and violence.

Jehu the Wordsmith: A Man of Few, but Manipulative, Words

Sometimes Jehu avoids having blood literally on his hands, and this introduces us to this third feature of has masculinity. Others have already demonstrated how persuasive speech is a valued expression of masculinity;[20] and while Jehu can be terse ("Him too, shoot!"; "throw her down!"), he is linguistically clever. To consolidate his reign, he instructs the guardians of Ahab's royal house to take the heads of their master's sons and meet him the next day. The instruction is ambiguous. "Heads" can literally mean the heads from their shoulders, or it can mean their leaders. The

---

18. Richard Nelson (1987, 205), for example, is a resistant reader when it comes to the "scope and brutality of Jehu's reforming violence" and ponders how far any deity could be "behind all this bloodshed and betrayal" (206). Robert Cohn (2000, 75–76) acknowledges that the problem with Jehu is that he "goes beyond the call of duty in his vehemence and deviousness."

19. Of course, the Hebrew Bible knows of women who kill, but note how gender norms are deliberately manipulated to masculinize characters such as Jael. On this, see Deborah Sawyer's (2002) excellent discussion.

20. Clines illustrates this in his studies of Moses, Aaron, David, and the prophets (1995, 2002, 2010). Brian DiPalma (2010) notes how persuasive speech can be a valued attribute of women in the Moses story. I agree, but I am uncomfortable with any suggestion that, if it is a valued womanly skill, it is not necessarily a marker of masculinity, for that reinforces notions of binary gender.

guardians, fearing for their lives, bring Jehu the literal heads, in seventy cooking pots (English translations soften the image by translating as "baskets," 2 Kgs 10:7). When Jehu subsequently accosts the public with an air of complete innocence, suggesting he has no idea where all these heads have come from, his capacity for deceptive language is overtly displayed. This is entirely consistent with Jehu's general ability to divert culpability, as noted by Wray Beal (2007, 73): Jehu "speaks and acts in such a way that he could always deflect responsibility and blame upon others." There are also the many examples of convenient, arguably manipulated oracles. Gina Hens-Piazza (2006, 293) notes, for example, how Jehu's declaration that Jezebel's excreted remains were a fulfillment of prophecy "exceeds the judgment and punishment of Jezebel specified in the original oracle." She rightly notes how "the question lurking in the minds of many readers intensifies: Was Jehu really fulfilling the word of the Lord spoken by the prophet, or was he fulfilling his own unbridled ambitions for power, no matter what the cost?" (297).

Robert Cohn (2000, 74) further notes the "guile" of this speech in Jehu's instruction to gather the Baal worshipers, who are dead if they come and dead if they do not. Jehu's speech can also be heavily ironic. Note the verbal wordplay at work in the scene that sets up the massacre of Baal worshipers. Jehu says that that he has a "great sacrifice" to offer in his service to Baal. But while Jehu says he will serve (עבד) Baal, the narrator informs the reader that he will actually destroy (אבד) Baal's worshipers.

Jehu's talk is reminiscent of the trickster, and his bloodshedding would cohere with the ways in which tricksterism operates in war contexts. Thus, although Susan Niditch (1993) deals with Jehu's revolution in her section on the ban as God's justice, the way Jehu goes about his assassinations is also consistent with her chapter on tricksterism, where battles are fought on the bases of deception and wit. A more overt sexual innuendo would be expected if Jehu was to be seen primarily as a trickster, but it is not entirely lacking. The Jehu narrative has its scatological elements, as noted particularly by Francisco García-Treto (1992), which encourage us to see its connection with the stories of Ehud, Jael, and Samson, and there is something rather erotic about his arrow shot, discussed further in the section below on phallic masculinity.

If being a man of few but effective words is allowed to congeal into a hegemonic norm, masculinity becomes characterized by brusque, manipulative forms of communication. Such forms might contain scatological humor but are amusing only if one is not on the deadly receiving end.

Jehu's double-edged conversation is used to cower other men into submission; it is a tool of domination, to wield authority. It is death-dealing, oppressively powerful, and, as part of the masculinity package, forges anew a connection with power and violence.

Jehu's Madness

While the *CBIC* depicts a stately, stable Jehu taking aim at Joram, 2 Kgs 9:20 says Jehu was recognizable by the way he drove his chariot—a manner variously translated as "furiously" (KJV), "like a madman" (GNB), or "like a maniac" (NRSV). Is the writer conjuring an image akin to the boy racers of today, known for expressing their masculinity through risk, speed, and competitiveness, or is Jehu's madness to be understood in terms of prophetic infection? The latter option is usually accepted on the basis of the root שגע, appearing twice in the narrative. The lad sent by Elisha to anoint Jehu is described by those looking on as משגע (2 Kgs 9:11).[21] The use of the same root to describe Jehu's driving convinces several commentators that Elisha's messenger has transferred his prophetic ecstatic behavior to Jehu.[22]

However, I am unconvinced by the contagion theory. Unlike the accounts of 1 Sam 19, here we are not given any overt notice that Jehu got caught up in the emissary's ecstasy or "madness." Even if we were to grant that it is an implied possibility, we would have to deal with the fact that it is a strangely delayed contagion, since Jehu appears to concur with his fellow officers that the lad was known for his "mad" conversation and acts with astute caution regarding the anointing and the reaction of his men.

---

21. For Cohn (2000, 66), this indicates that the lad "was seen as bizarre," while García-Treto (1992, 161) suggests that the messenger "is deliberately presented as a character of marginal, even risible status." Cogan and Tadmor (1988, 108) note the connection with 1 Sam 19:23–24, where Saul's messengers encounter prophets "in a frenzy," which infects the messengers, who themselves "fall into a frenzy." They appear to lose all sense of original mission so that Saul himself is obliged to travel to Naioth in Ramah, where he too falls under their prophetic display of "frenzy" and lies naked all night.

22. Leithart (2006, 220), Wray Beal (2007, 80), García-Treto (1992, 162), and Tomes (2003, 269) all argue that the lad's madness has infected Jehu. For Wray Beal (2007, 71) it is less about infection and more about Jehu's complete identification with the commission. In her view, Jehu has *become* the prophetic authority in his own story rather than being under the primary authority of another.

More tellingly, we learn of Jehu's madness entirely in connection with his reputation—*already gained*—for driving in this manner. It was *characteristic* of him to drive like this. Such a habit is not out of kilter with what we know about his fiery touch-paper temperament. Elisha tells his emissary to deliver the message, anoint Jehu, tie up his testicles, and run for it.[23] Elisha knows he is lighting a fuse.

Subsequently, the velocity of the narrative enhances the picture of an impetuous man by using verb strings. Wray Beal's (2007, 55) narrative approach highlights the effects of this grammatical device, noting how Jehu "appears in frenetic movement throughout the story moving it furiously along." Jehu's encounter with the horsemen sent out to meet him happens entirely on the hoof: "Jehu does not stop to discuss anything with the men; neither does he appear to slow his pace. The interchange takes place on the run … even as Jehu answers, he sweeps on toward his goal" (79). If there is a hint of prophetic contagion, Jehu has it firmly under control—using oracles, inventing oracles, to suit his purpose.[24] He acts with the calculation of one very much in his senses; ruthless, cold, devious, clearing out all who stand in the way of his fast track to the throne. So rather than fill in the narrative with ideas of contagion, what we can imply from the term's previous usage in relation to the emissary is that the madness of Jehu's driving is understood *pejoratively*. If, when used of prophetic behavior, it refers to "wild, uncontrolled behavior" (Cogan and Tadmor 1988, 108), we can make use of that implication without having to assume that Jehu fell afoul of infection. His driving is reckless, wild, aggressive.

Indeed, if charioteering is a chief measure of masculinity, then while Jehu is "doing man" well, he is also doing it with a twist—charioteering like a madman. Maybe, in the context of war, such charioteering was com-

---

23. "Tie up his testicles" is more generally rendered as "loin-girding," but Roland Boer convincingly argues that men are exhorted to do this, and it refers to binding up their testicles as part of the preparation for heading off somewhere. Indeed, the different references to how this was achieved indicates the man's "toughness and/or importance" (2012, 53). On Elisha's instruction to flee, note Iain Provan's (1995, 212) view that this instruction may well be due to Jehu's "reputation as something of a 'madman'" or because the reaction of the officers with Jehu cannot be second-guessed.

24. "Convenient" is a word often used by commentators in regard to Jehu's use of oracles. Nelson (1987, 202) wonders about the reminiscence Jehu offers to Bidkar, saying, "the reader has not encountered this particular oracle before" and that it seems "a bit too convenient." Savran's (1989, 153) view is that "there is something suspicious in the way Jehu conveniently has a divine oracle ready to defend his every action."

mendable, demonstrating a disregard for personal safety in order to rout the enemy (and the wider historical context of this narrative is the Aram-Damascus war). Maybe there was a tinge of admiration in the watchman's statement. But it seems more likely that Jehu had gained the reputation for irresponsible chariot driving, which would be more coherent with the pejorative use of שׁגע. Perhaps it indicates the kind of unrestrained, out-of-control masculinity that could endanger those with him as much as those against him.

Jehu's Phallic Masculinity

The alert to erotic undertones originally came from the *CBIC* illustration, in which Jehu aims his arrow at a curiously bent-over King Joram, who is looking back with anxiety from his own chariot. He has little chance of avoiding Jehu's penetrative arrow, and it is not heading for the space between his shoulders! I am reminded of Perry Nodelman's (2008, 77) insight into how the pictures within books "act as more complex shadows to them, providing the visual and emotional information about which the texts themselves remain silent." Whether the illustrators consciously posed the protagonists in such an overtly phallic scene is not known, but it is not entirely out of place. In rather a throwaway line, Northrop Frye (1982, 40) described Ahab's dynasty as an "effete" and "corrupt dynasty [that] was wiped out by Jehu in a whirlwind of righteous fury."[25] The implication is that Jehu's power is that of the aggressive, active man, while that of Joram is emasculated.

As for the text, 2 Kgs 9:24, which describes Jehu's arrow shot, does contain an unusual turn of phrase: Jehu (literally) "filled his hand with his bow." Given the euphemistic connotations of "arrow," "bow," and "hand," this verse is very resonant with phallic power and has an excess about it.[26] It is not merely that the narrator dwells on the shot with some kind of macabre "relish," reporting "in forensic style the exact path of the arrow"

---

25. Frye makes (1982, 40) this comment amid a discussion of the partisan nature of biblical reportage, comparing the Jehu of the text with the "abjectly submissive vassal" depicted in the Black Obelisk.

26. On how bows and arrows carry "phallic symbolism," see Hillers 1973, 73. On the euphemistic use of "hand," see Delcor 1967; and Bergman, von Sodon, and Ackroyd 1986. On the Assyrian and rabbinic usage of the "bow" to indicate male sexual potency, see Waldman 1978, 88.

(Cohn 2000, 68). Nor is it merely shorthand for some militaristic style of shot (Wray Beal [2007, 85] has Jehu drawing "the bow to its full extent"). The bow carries connotations of manly sexual vigor, and something more than just the literal loosing of an arrow seems to be lurking. Although it enters not Joram's buttocks but an area between his shoulders, coming out the other side, the entry of Jehu's "arrow" from the "bow" that filled his "hand" exudes an erotic scent.

Jehu's phallic masculinity is underscored by the scene at the Baal temple. García-Treto (1992, 163) brings this out well, noting how "Jehu's men will penetrate as far as the inmost recesses in order to bring outside the 'pillar of Baal.'" There are erotic undertones of penetrating an orifice, entering and castrating Baal by bringing out and destroying his "pillar." The surviving penises of the Israelites ensure that this location will henceforth be a latrine. Here is yet another interesting use of grammar: 10:27 contains the only feminine use of מחראה, usually translated "dung." Brueggemann (2000, 400) thus translates it "cesspool" or "latrine." The site of the temple, even in its destroyed state, bears the marks of having been feminized. Jehu's masculinity is a penetrative one that exerts supremacy over rival males and through whom Yhwh demonstrates his sovereignty over rival gods.

To summarize, the narrator's construction of Jehu's masculinity coheres, as one would expect, with the cultural norms that have been evidenced in other studies of biblical masculinities; that is, Jehu is female-avoidant (a man's man), violent, terse but with clever linguistic skills. In addition, the narrator implies a phallic masculinity and a rather disturbing edge of "madness." The close attention to masculinity brings into focus how extraordinary Jehu's story is; the narrator is in danger of representing an excessive performativity that prompts the reader to ponder how masculinity can run out of control and become repulsive rather than an invisible cultural norm. If we follow Judith Butler's (1990, 141) view that cases of extraordinary gender performativity undermine accepted gender polarities, then it is worth staying with those glimpses. The excessiveness reveals that supposedly innate gender categories are not inevitable, that indeed there is actually no essential grounding to them.

Herein lies one of the benefits of the transgender gaze. It observes keenly how masculinity is performed but inevitably stands at a distance from it, because ultimately there is that gap, that remoteness of not having being hailed in one's "maleness" from birth. The queer child, invested in an image of heroic, strong masculinity, finds the details of the text far less enviable. The jarring, repellent features stand out even more starkly, because that initial investment has been seriously undermined. The disappointment of a favored thing turning out flawed is always more greatly felt than if the thing had not been favored or desired in the first place. The magical aura is broken, the mystery is unraveled, and the exposure is viscerally felt. When the transgender gaze is also feminist, then the insights into the construction of Jehu's masculinity are given a still greater critical edge, as one is alert to how those feminist interests are compromised by the way masculinity is being configured.

Confronting Heteronormativity with Fragile, but Resilient, Alternative Visions of Gender

A common flaw in masculinity studies is the assumption that masculinity belongs to men. But masculinity is not a manifestation of biology. The transgender gaze announces that the emperor has no clothes—gendered categories have no ontological basis. It owns an alternative reality, the knowledge that the sex assigned at birth is not as essential as the regimes that apply it would like to believe. Masculinity can be a space occupied by the "girled" person who plays at being Troy Tempest in the street, by the drag kings who strut their stuff on the stage, by the butch lesbian, or by the FTM who occupies this ground.[27]

Yet this is also where the fragility of a transgender reading can be observed. Just as in street play a playmate might respond, "You can't be Troy Tempest, because you're just a girl," there is an insistence of the literal that counters the transgender gaze. Against it, the queer child asserts her own alternative reality: "No, I'm not a girl." The insistence on the literal also permeates the adult world, as seen in media obsession with "before and after" imagery. Prurient interest in the practice of transgender and

---

27. A girl, argues Butler (1993, 7–8), is not born a girl but is "girled" by those who pronounce "It's a girl" at birth and by the reinforcements that are subsequently applied. Cultural discourses sustain our sexed identity by requiring us at almost every turn to acknowledge it. But without the concept of "girl," body parts would not necessarily be imbued with such determinate meetings. Butler thus extends de Beauvoir's (1972, 295) argument that "one is not born, but rather becomes, a woman" by exposing how it is the regime of compulsory heterosexuality that demands binary gender, which in turn requires biological sex. Sex appears to be the foundation of gender, but Butler reverses that assumption.

transsexual transformation does not celebrate fluidity so much as remind readers of their gendered past and keep them pinned to it. Julia Serano (2007) reports how this has particularly been the case with MTF transitions; media interest is in how a body normatively hailed as "male" can display femininity with various measures of success. Their reports reassure the audience that this is an artificial "woman" constructed by surgery, costume, and learned gestures/behaviors. The trans woman might declare herself to be a woman, but the response remains, "You're not." The relevance to biblical interpretation is this: a transgender hermeneutic will always be on the back foot, because it has to assert itself in the face of the overwhelming strength of heteronormative assumptions. It will always be vulnerable to appeals to "common sense." It *is* therefore fragile and needs to be immensely defiant and resilient in staking its claim to its alternative knowledge. That is not to say that trans people insist on biological sameness with cisgendered identities. They are often the first to acknowledge that their transitioning identity is something different, that it places them in a location that we have few words for. They are *trans*. But even so, the determination to assert their own gender realities, rather than the ones to which they have been identified, remains strong.

A transgender reading is aware that none of the apparent markers of masculinity is inherently connected with a sexed body. Jehu is "doing man," and it is widely assumed that his gender performativity is not only congruent with his biological sex but an essential outworking of that. But the transgender gaze recognizes how the dint of sheer repetition solidifies expressions of gender into "maleness." Masculinity studies regrettably reinforce the connection by concentrating their efforts on analyzing male characters. Book titles such as *Men and Masculinity in the Hebrew Bible and Beyond* (Creangă 2010) do little to unhinge the supposed link between sex and gender. Interventions are needed quite urgently in order to disturb this trend. By focusing on *Jehu's* performance of masculinity, in the discussion (thus far) I have played into those sex/gender assumptions.

So in order to unpack masculinity from sexed bodies, I shift attention to Jezebel to explore how masculinity is configured in this character. If masculinity is a cultural space into which one can step, then the way she strides across the books of Kings with agency, acumen, and audacity, competing with the masculinity of other players, merits attention. Following Judith Halberstam (1998), one might write about this under the heading of "female masculinity"—a phrase that confronts readers with a usefully destabilizing contradiction. I appreciate that this may be a problematic phrase for those who are uncomfortable with terminology that draws attention to "female." If they have spent their lives shifting out of that category, they do not want to be reified as female all over again. That said, Cromwell's work on trans men repeatedly refers to "female-bodied" trans men, making the point that trans men will always carry some mark of being female-bodied,[28] and that this is the distinctive thing they bring to their inhabitation of the masculine. Ultimately, I concur that the reference to "female-bodied" trans men does helpfully open up a discussion of gender diversity and, more significantly, challenges assumptions that the penis makes the man. The trans man may have affinities for the style culturally associated with "men"; but, in inhabiting that space as *female-bodied trans men*, the essentialist notion of "man/woman" is troubled.

With these points in mind, we now turn our attention to Jezebel's presence in this narrative. In 2 Kgs 9, Jezebel steps on to the stage only to die, but some significant threads in these few verses are worthy of comment. I limit myself to three points: (1) Jezebel occupies "masculine" space; (2) Jezebel is deliberately feminized; and (3) the connection of Jezebel with the goddess enhances, rather than undermines, the portrayal of female masculinity.

JEZEBEL'S OCCUPATION OF MASCULINE SPACE

In the reception history are several nods to how Jezebel's defiant use of language, hailing Jehu as a "Zimri," can readily be associated with the masculine. Claudia Camp (1992, 103) is the most overt, referring to Jezebel's "masterful" verbal skills. Judith McKinlay (2004, 80) talks of Jezebel's "battle taunt." John Gray (1977, 551) refers to the defiance in her greeting with its "well chosen … invective in her reference to Zimri." Cogan and Tadmor (1988, 112) refer to Jezebel's "self-assurance and courage." Hens-Piazza (2006, 292) notes how Jezebel takes the initiative—preparing to meet Jehu with as much dignity as can be mustered, drawing on "self-reliance" and pride. Wray Beal (2007, 91) describes the greeting as one of "haughty scorn" but extends this to a suggestion that Jezebel may have

---

28. For example, "scars, an inability to have spontaneous erections, and (for most) a lack of sensation in the penile shaft, the insertion of a prosthetic device for intercourse, and an inability to urinate through the penis" (Cromwell 1999, 29).

entertained "hopes of cowing him by her presence."[29] Indeed, she suggests that Jezebel's address "introduces a moment of doubt" (93) for those listening. Could Jehu's reign similarly be over within seven days? Might Jehu meet a similar fate to the self-immolation of Zimri? Of course, we know that it turns out differently, but there is a momentary chink of suspense for the reader, who might contemplate whether Jehu's ruthless, violence masculinity with his manipulative use of language may have met its match and indeed be defeated by Jezebel's superior display of masculine strength (she does, after all, have a reputation for killing all the prophets of Yhwh). Jezebel's masculinity is thus seen in her final sentence that at least matches Jehu's linguistics for tone and irony.

To those who would criticize this association of Jezebel's strength of speech with masculinity, who, perhaps for feminist reasons, want to reclaim this as a female strength, I request that they consider the erasing nature of that act. I understand the rationale for the move: there are few enough images of strong, resistant, independent women in the Hebrew Bible, and we do not want to surrender Jezebel's qualities to the "masculine." But the history of female masculinity has been one of repeated erasure and marginalization, and I want to enhance rather than hide the embodiment that is on display in this text. The trans gaze finds here an image it can relate to, an image of awesome female masculinity. While feminists have few enough images that are worth redeeming, the trans person's cache is even less populated. This scene between Jezebel and Jehu is a power struggle, and we have competing masculinities on display. Let us not lose sight of that.

Offsetting that view, however, is the reference to Jezebel facing Jehu with painted eyes and having done something to her head/hair. Surely these are the actions of a woman, drawing strongly on her femininity—as memorably depicted in the painting *Jezebel* by John Byam Liston Shaw (1896), who introduces a mirror to add to the narcissistic effect. However, the section below explains this as a framing technique that deliberately tames the female masculinity on display.

---

29. This view derives from Jezebel's verbal play combined with the attempt to overawe Jehu by her choice of makeup, demonstrating royal dignity.

The Feminization of Jezebel

What exactly Jezebel does is not easy to perceive. She applies a product, usually translated as "antimony," to her eyes, and she "makes pleasing/adorns" (יתב) her head. Whatever this involved, Jezebel usually stands accused of using the accoutrements of femininity and sexuality to address Jehu. Simon Parker's (1978) view, that Jezebel uses her makeup and womanly vices in order to seduce Jehu, is generally rejected, but the hint of erotic purpose has not gone away. Peter Leithart (2006, 221) suggests that she decks herself out "as if to welcome a John." Cohn (2000, 69) does not allude to prostitution but does reinforce femininity in his description: "primping in her boudoir, preparing for his arrival.... She paints, pretties, and peers out of her window."

Janet Gaines (1999, 79) asks us to reconsider the age of Jezebel when she was assassinated—around fifty—"well past her nubile prime." The antimony and whatever she did to her head has, in Gaines's view, far more to do with dignity and royal strength/pride: "Her conduct is heroic. Cool and composed, Jezebel adorns her face and arranges her hair before she proceeds to the upper window to meet certain death" (87). The suggestion that Jezebel plays on her royalty in this scene is borne out by the fact that antimony was a luxury item; it is an indicator of wealth and social status.[30]

But why would the Deuteronomist, who is virulently anti-Jezebel, create an image of dignity and strength? It seems contradictory to imagine that he permits, at the end, some admiration of her royal display. Given that painted eyes do not have a good press elsewhere in the Hebrew Bible (Jer 4:30; Ezek 23:40), it is more convincing to understand Jezebel's actions in terms of deliberate Deuteronomistic criticism. McKinlay (2004, 81) suggests, for example, that we could read the references to her toilet as a concerted attempt to offset the disturbing effect of Jezebel's authority. In a context where war and politics were largely the preserves of men, this powerful queen mother stands as a disturbing anomaly. As it was commonplace to feminize and castrate an enemy, the powerfulness of Jezebel is tempered by emphasizing her womanly toilet. If this is so, then Jezebel's female masculinity is thus purposefully emasculated.

---

30. For further discussion of cosmetic usage in the ancient Near East, see Thompson 1962, 202–3; Koosed 2006, 178; and Matthews 2006, 754–55.

McKinlay mentions the attendant likelihood that Jezebel is criticized for breaking out of the bounds of her femaleness, and her fall becomes pedagogical for all women:

> I am meant to be shocked by the dissonance of a woman with all her femininity displayed being apparently engaged in a military encounter and uttering battle taunts. The writer wants his readers to understand that while this is indeed a woman in all the feminine senses, this is one who has not acted her part as a woman in Israel, and women who do not behave like women—according to this narrator's gender construction—must fall from their place. Crossing boundaries, including gender boundaries, has fateful, even deathly, consequences; such people must be removed for the health and wellbeing of the greater good. (2004, 81–82)

In either scenario, what is clear to a trans reader is that female masculinity is too hard to bear. It has to be contained, eliminated, emasculated. Yet the Deuteronomist is in a double bind. By demonstrating the dangers of female masculinity, he inevitably gives us sight of it. Compared with Jezebel's (and Jehu's), the other performances of masculinity in 2 Kgs 9–10 pale into insignificance. The eunuchs, far from manning up to the challenge of the usurper, comply immediately with Jehu's instruction. They are "decidedly not of the stuff of Jezebel" (McKinlay 2004, 82).[31] The coexisting masculinities on display in this narrative are like bland watercolors against the richly painted Jehu and Jezebel. Those displayed by the eunuchs, Elisha, the overthrown kings, and their retinue hardly compete. It is Jezebel who, at last, is someone prepared to take the fight to Jehu, issuing her contemptuous taunt from the window. It is Jezebel who "mans up."

---

31. I do not concur with the evaluation of Jehu's masculinity in Kolakowski's essay, but she has interesting views on how the eunuchs might function as "mediators of the gender play between the defiant, seductive and strong Jezebel and the dubiously manly Jehu" (2000, 107). Kolakowski questions whether their jettison of Jezebel may have been a way of "symbolically regaining their masculinity" (108) or whether the eunuchs have to enable the victory because the Israelites have become so impotent that they are incapable and "need the assistance of half-men, most likely foreigners" (108). Kolakowski leaves these and other options open.

Jezebel and the Elimination of the Goddess

Jezebel's appearance at a window brings to mind the ivory plaques unearthed in Samaria that depict a frontal female face, with Hathor-styled hair; McKinlay (2004, 88) argues that "the destruction of Jezebel may also have been represented as a shattering of the goddess Hathor/Asherah herself."[32] If it was the case that queen mothers were seen as the earthly counterpart of the goddess, then perhaps this was "the source of her power" (89). If so, then the command to throw her down is double-voiced, echoing Deuteronomistic instructions to cut down the Asherah. So "there is now a double dimension in view, for the window dispatch is not only the tipping out of an earthly human queen but also the degrading and bringing down to earth of a queen who embodies the sacred" (89). If this is right, and Jezebel is a figurative representation of the goddess, then it is her femininity, not masculinity, that seems to come to the fore—indeed, a femininity writ large.

But the text of 2 Kgs 9 does not actually refer to Jezebel's hair, only to her "head" that she makes attractive. I am thus not so persuaded that the connection is to Hathor and ultimately to Asherah. There *is*, however, a possible connection to Anat, as nodded to by Deborah Appler (2006). The strange reference to the body parts that remain of Jezebel after the trampling of her body—her skull and feet and the palms of her hands—is so specific that perhaps the narrator is conveying something in particular. In *KTU* 1.3.ii.12–15, Anat butchers enemy soldiers on the battlefield, hangs their heads on her back, and attaches their palms to her sash/waist. William Dever (2005, 270) gets the imagery of this text across very viscerally: Anat is a hunter and "warrior goddess who rounds up Ba'al's enemies and slaughters them, wading up to her vulva in blood and gore, laughing triumphantly." Anat is as bloody as Jehu—a wild and furious warrior. If there could be a deliberate implied connection with the myth of Anat, then the image of goddess that is conjured is not one of femininity writ large, but one of undoubted female masculinity. Bear in mind, for instance, how Anat is described, in Papyrus Chester Beatty VII 1.9–2.1, as "a mighty goddess, a woman acting as a man/a warrior, clad as men, girt like women" (D. Sweeney 2011, 3). Further, Anat's masculinity features strongly in the Aqhat epic, where she strongly desires its primary symbol—the bow fash-

---

32. On the association between Hathor and Asherah, she cites Hadley (2000, 9, 47, 161) and Ackerman (1998, 178).

ioned by Kothar-wa-Hasis, and arrows—and is mightily infuriated when the bow is denied. For Delbert Hillers (1973), this can be understood symbolically, that is, that Anat is threatening to emasculate Aqhat by appropriating his "bow." Peggy Day nuances this by suggesting that Anat's appropriation of male symbols needs to be read against her status as *btlt*. Anat is "suspended in the liminality of adolescence, where male and female social roles have not yet been fully differentiated … so she is 'free' to participate in the culturally masculine pursuits of warfare and hunting" (1992, 183). A connection with the goddess Anat would, therefore, reinforce the image of female masculinity.

But before there can be any celebration of this, we need to bear in mind that we are witnessing the destruction of Jezebel/a goddess. There is no celebration of a gender-crossing divine. The palms and skulls that Anat freely slings around her person are now Jezebel's own. The blood and gore in which Anat once walked knee-deep is also now Jezebel's own. If Anat is the "Mistress of Animals" proposed by P. Day (1992), then there is bitter irony in that animals—dogs—consume Jezebel. In short, I concur that we may be witnessing the elimination of the goddess but that it is *Anat's female masculinity* that is being overthrown.

If it is overreaching to suggest that the reference to head, hands, and feet are meant to conjure an image of Anat, then these body parts still remain symbols of power. In Danna Fewell and David Gunn's view, they remain the parts of a "powerful and independent woman"; but it is that image of the powerfully independent woman that is so alarming for the narrator. Indeed, it simply "*cannot be*, so it must be unmade, in mocking fashion, leaving its symbols of power, in bizarre independence, without a woman's torso to signal unambiguously that they are a woman's" (1993, 171, emphasis added).

If we reflect on the above section as a whole, the alternative vision of gender produced in this trans reading is that those hailed as "girls" or "women" can traverse gender norms and play the man as well as those expected to be male/masculine. I am not averse to the view that Jezebel uses female strength. I do not deny that point in order to make her into some transgender hero. What I *do* want to argue in this section is that Jezebel must be included in any discussion of performative masculinities. Not to do so risks reifying the connection of gender to supposedly fixed biology.

I returned to the *CBIC* wondering if I had missed the depiction of Jezebel's last stand. After all, I had largely ignored the representations of women in the *CBIC* as background fodder. Mostly doe-eyed and feminine, they bore little or no appeal. Even characters like Jael are lamentably depicted (a soft, gentle-looking, demure young woman hands her bowl of milk to the far more appealing Sisera). But Jezebel's last stand is dramatic—one worthy of a double-page spread. Could it be that I had forgotten a depiction of the defiant, magnificent Jezebel standing at the window, issuing her battle cry? No; she was not there. I am reminded of McKinlay's argument that the defiance (in my terms, the masculinity) of Jezebel is too much for the Deuteronomist and his readers. It has to be eliminated.

POLITICAL ENGAGEMENT:
THE EFFECTS OF THIS ACT OF BIBLICAL INTERPRETATION

It is difficult to know how far the biblical narrator endorses Jehu. If we focus strongly on the all-too-convenient oracles, his bloodthirstiness, the loss of territory, the restriction of his dynasty to four generations, and the observation that Jehu too walked in the ways of Jeroboam, we could argue that the narrator implicitly criticizes Jehu. Cohn (2000, 76), for instance, believes that Jehu receives the narrator's praise for the elimination of the Baal cult, but that while his "laudable end is thus praised, Jehu's methods are severely criticized." But other commentators are less convinced. Cogan and Tadmor (1988, 119) say that it is "difficult to find the 'implicit protest' against Jehu and his supporters that some scholars have found in these chapters," adding that "2 Kings 9–10 relates the events without judgment." This raises the uncomfortable thought that the Deity (via the narrator) does indeed sanction all Jehu's actions, and some commentators face this square on: Leithart (2006, 223) notes that Jehu is the only northern king said to have done well and what was right in God's eyes, thereby comparing him favorably to David and suggesting that Jehu's zeal "provides a model for the great reforming kings of Judah." G. H. Jones (1984, 450) also identifies Deuteronomistic approval. Most commentators, however, opt for ambiguity and say that the narrator's evaluation of Jehu is "equivocal." There are some clear markers of the narrator's praise, as seen in the note that Jehu fulfills all that is in Yhwh's heart (10:30), but there are also the troubling features of the text. Brueggemann (2000, 400), for example, says there are two cheers for Jehu, but "before a third can be added … along comes v. 29. This verse is negative and qualifies v. 28." Yet, at the end of his commentary, Brueggemann also questions Yhwh's complicity with shameless violence (403) and warns readers today that "violence driven by religious passion becomes a terrible enterprise" (404).[33]

But it is not the biblical narrator's evaluation alone that warrants scrutiny—it is our own. Hens-Piazza (2006, 293–94) stands out most effectively as a commentator calling her readers to consider the ethics of 2 Kgs 9–10, noting how we are "enlisted or even co-opted to assent to this violence and to the condemnation of those earmarked for blame." Given how it is all too easy to read with the grain of a biblical text and vilify the outsider, Hens-Piazza calls us

> to reconsider those identified as the "Jezebels" of our own world: those who suffer the violence of sustained or disproportionate blame; those who incur damaged reputations because of their gender, ethnic identity, or their status as "other"; and those who are excoriated for their wrongdoings and are deemed undeserving of forgiveness. (296)

I doubt that Hens-Piazza had transgender people in mind when she wrote her commentary, but they have been targets for the kind of oppression she describes. A trans reading cannot fail to note how female masculinity is part of that othering process or how the "woman" who subverts gender norms can be punished by death. When McKinlay (2004, 84) shifts her attention to what the murder of Jezebel signifies, she suggests that it supplies an overt clue about "what Israel wants eliminated from its midst." Jezebel thus operates a cypher for the assertion of Israelite identity: "she is to be the measure of what they are not" (84). But, as McKinlay perceives, the consequences of this "reach far beyond the world of the houses of Ahab and Jehu," for "this is one of the many stories told over time and in many places to justify the rejection of the Other, and as such adds to their force" (94). Bearing in mind how the murder of Brandon began our theorizing of the transgender gaze, the interpreter has a moral obligation to consider how this trans "other" can become a site for forceful rejection/elimination.

So I return to a point I argued in my chapter on Genesis: the "normal" preserve their normality by projecting monstrous "freakishness" on the other. Here too we have a story of polar opposites: the prophets, Jehu,

---

33. Marvin Sweeney's (2007, 339) source-critical reading solves the ambiguity by identifying the "propagandist" tenor of the earlier text, which declared divine support for Jehu's action and legitimated the slaughter, while Hezekian and Josianic later editions qualified that praise.

and Yhwh versus Jezebel and Baal. But as Trible's (1995, 179) essay demonstrates, "In Elijah, Jezebel resides; in Jezebel, Elijah resides"; they are "mirror images" and "inextricably hinged through the convergence of opposites." The righteousness of the Yhwh group is violently defined by maligning and eliminating the Baal group, but their inextricable connection with each other cannot be expunged.

Trible's astute attention to the hopelessness of trying to eject that which is Other is also noted by Fewell and Gunn in their discussion of Jezebel. While the politics of the text favors casting out the foreign Other who can insidiously seduce Israel away from her exclusive bond to Yhwh, she cannot be cast out as entirely separate from Israel, she cannot be so easily eliminated. "She has fertilized the fields. Her body has been consumed by generations of Israelites. Her flesh is their flesh. To disgorge Jezebel, Israel must be disgorged. So the subject narrates, with approval, his own dissipation. Only thus can the fearful, female, alien, Other be truly kept at bay" (1993, 184).

Only when we refrain from indulging our anxieties about the other, which will always be our anxieties about ourselves, can there really be any shalom. Only when the Jehu script of ring-fencing masculinity by female-avoidant attitudes and behavior is dismantled will there be a balance of animus and anima that enables us to move forward with one another in tolerance and mutual understanding. Only when there is freedom for the fluidity of gender to exist can we stop condemning transsexuality and transgender and see, in ourselves, the fluidity that we so fear.

In this, there is also something for trans communities to consider. The border wars, discussed above, can fall prey to female-avoidant anxieties. Cromwell (1999, 28–29) notes how some of his participants self-identify as trans men in order "to distance themselves from anything that connotes female or feminine." I understand this separation, finding it difficult myself to associate with words like *woman, feminine.* However, I would be unwilling to encourage any cultural understanding of masculinity as a ring-fenced zone, uncontaminated from women or the feminine. I am more in favor of Cromwell's view that while FTM individuals might share affinities for the behaviors, dress, and cultural ideas associated by essentialist discourses with "men," in inhabiting that space as female-bodied transmen, the essentialist notion of "man/men" is troubled. Cromwell himself does not identify as "man": "For appearances sake, I am a man. But I'm not an ordinary man. Never could be and never will be" (1999, 127).

So, there is a tangible difference between female-avoidant male-defined masculinity and the person, hailed as a woman, wishing to liberate "herself" from the encumbrance and alienation that this imposed identity poses. Another difference, I argue, is that the transitioning person, while disowning the identity, can remain emphatically pro-woman and feminist. The pro-woman, feminist, adult Deryn can no longer look at the image of Jehu in the *CBIC* with the same admiration as the queer child, who saw in his taut skin and tanned muscles an image of desirable masculinity. The textual Jehu embodied a masculinity that comes at a very high price—one that I am not willing to pay. Jehu's masculine performativity is not something I could ever endorse.

When considering our ethical responsibility as hermeneuts, we cannot neglect Namaste's (2009) injunction to consider how far transgender and transsexual people's lives are enhanced, or their interests served, by the results of academic theorizing. My hope is that this book brings to the fore the need for trans hermeneutics and creates the kind of knowledge that can be useful for trans people. Specifically, I hope that it will help to expose the ways in which gender is constructed in biblical texts and the mechanisms by which the "other" is demonized. Namaste (2009, 23) calls for greater inclusion of "indigenous knowledge" in academic work, rather than such work contributing to a reobjectifying of trans people. I have delved deeply into my own trans affinities in order to write this chapter while drawing widely on the work of trans discourses and experiences. More work is needed, not least because trans is constructed differently depending on location, ethnicity, class, and all those other intersections and crossroads that affect our definitions and understandings. The model advocated in this discussion will inevitably be limited, constrained by the experiences of queerness in my own life and context. But at its heart are the interests of trans people who are still accosted by Bible-brandishing figures of influence.

In addition, I hope this work demonstrates the need for all biblical scholars to consider the effects of their work for those who do not occupy the institutionally privileged sites of binary gender. I want to expand the project of biblical hermeneutics and call for a more interdisciplinary approach to interpreting biblical texts where trans discourses are engaged, alongside queer and feminist discourses. This would enrich our discipline and, one hopes, make it more accountable to the people for whom the Bible continues to be used as an instrument of oppression.

Conclusion

There has been something perversely pleasurable about discussing my queer negotiations with the *CBIC* and how occupying the space given to male characters was a way of affirming a queer, fluid self. That childhood enjoyment and identification with images of masculinity seem coherent with the queerness that Alexander Doty (1993, xv) describes as "an attitude, a way of responding, that begins in a place not concerned with, or limited by, notions of a binary opposition of male and female or the homo versus hetero paradigm." Although the adult Deryn rears back from Jehu's repulsive masculinity, the opportunity to follow up on that early alignment and work out a model of trans engagement with a biblical text has been informative and challenging. It has been particularly gratifying to make one's way into a text that is not knowingly set up to facilitate trans engagement. As Melynda Huskey (2002, 69) perceives, "by moving our interpretive venture outside the round dozen or so of explicitly gay picture books to the innumerable theoretically 'nongay' picture books, we stake a claim much more unsettling to the status quo." I would argue that, when it comes to such a culturally influential text as the Bible, the challenge to the status quo is even more unsettling and controversial.

So what does an FTM reading achieve? It provides a close analysis of gender performativity; it is feminist-aware; it acknowledges the fluidity of subject positions in the reader; it does not objectify supposed trans people but puts the spotlight on existing gender norms. It is astutely aware of masculinity as a cultural space and that FTM readers come with different ideas about how the world might operate. It has to deal with the potential for disdaining the feminine. It demonstrates how the interpreter, hailed originally as "woman" but choosing to occupy territory associated with "man," does masculinity with a different set of experiences. These experiences inform how and what a trans reader is peculiarly equipped to bring to the interpretive table. And the work is culturally important. Nodelman (2008, 173) argues that one of the important colonizing aspects of children's literature is that "it intends to teach what it means for girls to be girls and boys to be boys," because ensuring "that children understand culturally significant differences between males and females remains a significant goal in the socialization of children" (173). If that is so, then applying the trans gaze to biblical texts is a vital new hermeneutical lens that can offset the heteronormative ends to which biblical texts are often put and provide a counterdiscourse to those who use the Bible to denounce transgender or transsexual persons.

4

THE DANCE OF GENDER: DAVID, JESUS, AND PAUL*

Teresa J. Hornsby

Those lines in the sand are made to cross over, and that crossing—as every nomadic subject knows, constitutes who we are. (Butler 2004, 203)

The topic of gender transition is one that many of us (usually Western-trained Bible scholars) find to be too theoretical, too ethereal, and not connected to "real" scholarship—you know, history, language, and such. But this is the magic trick, the great abracadabra that traditional Bible scholarship has pulled off: pay no attention to the whimsy of gender scholarship—it is irrelevant at best; it has no real value; pay no attention to that gender theorist behind the curtain! I plan to challenge the notion that gender is tangential and abstract, is of no real consequence, and has no concrete connection to the New Testament's history.[1] I will argue that a two-sexed,

---

* This is a revision of a chapter that was previously published as Hornsby 2014 and is used by permission of the editor.

1. While gender studies has become more pervasive and more credible in Bible scholarship over the last thirty years, it remains an oddity and is seen, as evidenced by the number of publications, public presentations, and academic courses, as tangential to "real" Bible studies. For example, of the 110 program units at the 2014 International Annual Meeting of the Society of Biblical Literature and the European Association of Biblical Studies, 6 units address gender as their primary focus (though I would not equate a gendered focus with gender theory, I have included those units here). Of the 203 program units offered at the 2014 Annual Meeting of the Society of Biblical Literature, 6 are directly concerned with gender. Of course, in some of these other units there may be a paper that may use gender theory. There is no group, however, specifically appointed to discuss Paul and gender or gender theory and the Bible, for example. On the same note, just because a unit may be titled, "Women in the Biblical World," it does not necessarily mean the papers presented there would use gender

gender binary is the absolute foundation upon which early Christian communities are built: Paul relies on them to make his fledgling group distinct from the greater Roman mainstream, and the early church relied on them to maintain church hierarchical structures. However, I would like to propose here that it is possible to read some of Jesus's sayings in a way that suggests that Jesus does envision a community in which boundaries, though still in place, are much more flexible, and thus possibly transitional.

In this essay, I will think through the tense intersections of gender and sexuality, with the idea that these two aspects are somehow static and "God-given." Particularly, I am curious to see how one might use examples from the New Testament to talk about modern notions of gender transition.

For a few years, I have been working and thinking about boundaries, as well as crossing them. I think about this in terms of "real" boundaries, that is, geographical borders, the skin of the body, the rules that determine membership. I have been thinking about those abstract, malleable, fluid boundaries: gender, race, class, and so on. I will dwell on two points primarily: First, there is, of course, no "real" boundary—every wall, every border, is constructed; each holds the means of its dissolution. Second, no border is fixed—all are dynamic and malleable. I understand "boundaries"

---

theory (see "Meetings," n.d.). In the metropolitan area of Springfield, Missouri, where I live, seven postsecondary institutions offer courses on the Bible: Central Bible College, Assemblies of God Seminary, Evangel College, Drury University, Missouri State University, Baptist Bible College, and Southwest Bible University. Of these seven, only two offer courses specifically on gender theory and the Bible: Drury University and Missouri State University. I understand that this is anecdotal evidence at best and is but a small sample from an extremely conservative part of the United States; however, in the Chicago metropolitan area, eleven institutions make up the Association of Chicago Theological Schools (ACTS): Bexley Seabury, Catholic Theological Union, Chicago Theological Seminary, Garrett Evangelical Seminary, Lutheran School of Theology, McCormick Theological Seminary, Meadville Lombard, Northern Seminary, North Park Theological Seminary, Trinity Evangelical Divinity School, and Mundelein Seminary. Of these, three offer a course specifically on gender theory and the Bible (Chicago Theological, McCormick, and Lutheran Theological). Granted, a few offer courses such as "Women in the Old Testament," which one could argue concerns "gender" as a focus, but the course descriptions give no indication that any attention is paid to gender as a social construction, the intersections of gender and power, or any concern beyond the historical presence of women. To refer to those types of courses as "gender theory" would be akin to calling a course on personal finance "economic theory." My point is, among hundreds of biblical studies courses, there is precious little attention given to gender theory proper.

in the sense that Mary Douglas (1966) so brilliantly illustrated: Western cultures seek to delineate differences by dualistic categorization: everything must fit neatly and precisely into one and only one group. Any ambiguity is perceived as a threat and is deemed to be dangerous.

Douglas illustrates her ideas through the example of the Levitical codes in the Hebrew Bible. She argues that the Israelites understood themselves to be one body, and by governing the orifices (mouth and genitals) and the borders (the skin) of that body, they were shoring up any potential points of community vulnerability. The implication is that any infraction of laws that govern the body (which is a symbolic microcosm of the Israelite world) opens up the entire community to potential destruction. The prophets, then, understood the invasion, destruction, and forced exile of Israel (and Judah) to be consequences of neglected and eroded boundaries. The apostle Paul understood the body's boundaries and the fledgling Christian community's borders in exactly the same way.[2]

Just as the Israelites and the diasporic Jewish communities (indeed, any group who seeks to create an identity) sought to etch out a distinct identity among the nations, Paul's primary task was creating a community that was defined over and against the greater Roman community and the political rebellions of the kingdom of God movements. Paul, diasporic Jew that he was, accepted the idea (though, perhaps, not the specifics) behind the purity codes. Paul assumed that "soft" and malleable borders, borders that were ambiguous and dynamic, presented a real threat to the survival of this group. Paul's task was more complicated, however, than simply fortifying his communal walls. While, on the one hand, he sought to reinforce the boundaries that defined Christians, on the other hand, a primary theme throughout his letters is the dissolution of many of the codes upon which community formation happens (for example, the idea that some foods are unclean and the body has a special mark, i.e., circumcision, that makes it a distinctive body). The central symbol for the Christian community is no longer a generic body whose entrances, borders, and exits have to be regulated but the body of Christ. Yet, while food

---

2. As it has developed out of Levi-Strauss's structuralist anthropological theory, Mary Douglas's scholarship on boundary construction provides a foundation for recent work on the intersections of gender and the New Testament. Two studies that expound on Paul's community building and boundary concerns are Countryman 1988 and Martin 1999.

and circumcision are no longer acceptable markers of distinction, sex and, therefore, gender are.

As Paul moves away from the Judaic purity regulations regarding food, he relies heavily upon Western ideas regarding sex and gender. Paul builds this community upon two illusions, illusions that continue to be the foundation of Western culture: that there are two, and only two, complementary genders, and that these two genders are fixed. What is then assumed about the fixedness of gender is that gender is determined by nature (or God) and is inextricably connected to the body (which is also fixed).

Thus, it follows, if we believe that the two genders are "natural" or "God-given," that any expression of gender that does not conform to the predetermined sets of actions allowed to that body is considered to be odd—not a neutral or benign odd (if there is such a thing), but one that is morally weighted.[3] As Judith Butler (1988, 521) famously writes, "indeed, those who fail to do their gender right are regularly punished." "Performing right" usually means, first and foremost, having sexual desire for the opposite sex. Everything else stems from that desire, for example, wearing the correct clothing, proper adornment of one's hair, eating the correct food, riding the appropriate bicycle, or watching television suitable to one's gender.

This dominant belief system concerning sexuality that relies on fixed and binary genders and on the certainty that heterosexuality is the norm that occurs naturally, that is, apart from cultural influences, is called *heteronormativity*. All other sexual relationships are deemed culturally produced (unnatural), are regulated and defined in relation to heterosexuality, and are thus devalued. In this system, females and males are assumed to be the only appropriate sexual partners.

Heterosexism, then, is a systematic social bias, which stems from heteronormativity, in which society rewards heterosexuals (in the form of economic benefits and civil rights) and punishes all other sexualities. Like the air we breathe, heteronormativity and heterosexism are pervasive yet invisible; it is an assumed and unquestioned notion that there are only two naturally occurring and opposite sexes, and each is, naturally, attracted to the other. This heterosexual desire is created and blessed by a deity. These

---

3. Bernadette Brooten (1996) gives a thorough exploration of first-century attitudes regarding gender and sexuality.

assumptions then dictate that there are only two genders. Hence, any and every expression of gender that does not "match" one's assigned physical sex is rendered deviant; any sexual desire not directed to one's opposite sex is aberrant. This aberrance is interpreted as sin or as unnatural, which justifies punishment and violence against anyone who does not conform to this paradigm.

Heteronormativity is a culturally produced ideology, justified and maintained institutionally through religious beliefs, economic and political systems, medical classifications, psychiatric diagnoses, and judicial processes (Foucault 1978). The dominant premise of heteronormativity permeates every detail of one's life: love, marriage, aging, death, reproduction, property ownership, leisure time, and so on. Only in recent times has the "natural" occurrence of heteronormativity been challenged, and with this recognition has come a chipping away of the mighty fortresses of heterosexism. For example, in recent New Testament scholarship, scholars have dissected Paul's language in the Letter to the Romans to understand how he and his contemporaries perceive the term "natural" and how he uses this understanding to deem some desires as "against nature" (παρὰ φύσιν) (Brooten 1996). Most of us no longer consider the naturalness of gender in the same way that Paul did (for example, for a man to clip his hair short is God's preferred style of hair, or if a woman does not wear a head covering she would be acting unnaturally and against God), yet many of us are also not quite ready to completely jettison the idea that some things about gender are "natural." Specifically, not many would so readily question that women are *born* to be good mothers, or that men, because of their biology, are simply better suited for combat situations. How many of us would hesitate to say (or, perhaps, have never considered) that having sexual desire for the opposite sex might be no more natural (or unnatural) than having an attraction to someone of the same sex?

Nonetheless, every gendered detail is equally weighted. *All* of these assumptions about gender (whether it seems "inconsequential"—like what color clothes should a baby wear—or matters of prime importance: are men *naturally* better at leading nations and corporations?) are all equally critical and are relentlessly fed to us through various cultural institutions. The one cultural institution that we are most interested in today is Christianity and the interpretations of the New Testament; interpretation is an essential device in the gender-normative tool kit.

The inextricable connection of gender to our bodies (and thus our bodies' chemical and biological makeup) has long been taken as, well, the gospel "truth"—that because of natural, God-given drives, men desire women and women desire men, primarily in order to reproduce—that is our destiny. To accept this premise unquestionably (i.e., that gendered actions—including sexual desires—are naturally connected to our genitals) concretizes the notion that some bodies are better than others. To understand gender as static, unmoving, is to say that there is no hope for real change. If we continue to hold on to the notion that there are only two genders and two sexes, and all subsequent gendered behaviors are natural, thus unchanging, then lasting social and political change is impossible, because it is anchored to nature. Thus, to study gender and gender theory is not inconsequential or ethereal or tangential to "real" scholarship—apart from gender theory and the dismantling of "the big lie" of its naturalness, there is no point in doing any other kind of scholarship, because in the end, nothing really changes.

Then my task as a scholar of New Testament studies, one that is firmly planted in historical methods, in translation of ancient languages, and in the social sciences, is twofold: (1) to uncover the ways in which we (academics, products of a Westernized discipline) are accomplices in reproducing these lies about sex and gender for the masses (that gender is natural, stable, and dualistic); and (2) to uncover (to reveal, as in ἀποκάλυψις) the ways the New Testament shows us alternatives to our misperceptions about gender.

My project here is this: as Douglas and others explain, boundaries are necessary for community building (and gender is the foundation of all boundaries), but boundary dissolution and boundary crossing are equally necessary (e.g., Foucault). I want to explore the idea of using "dance" as a heuristic model for gender variability and transition. Dance is simultaneously physical, culturally determined, dynamic, and delightful. Yet its determination cannot be left in isolation from the body. Consider the following case of a short-lived dance movement that emerged in Greenwich Village in New York City in the 1960s.

DANCE: GREENWICH VILLAGE 1960–1970

Roughly between 1960 and 1970, a dance movement erupted in Manhattan's Greenwich Village. Inspired by the question, what is dance?, the dancers answered, what *isn't* dance? This group of dancers, sometimes referred to as Judsonites because of the performance space, "rejected codified dance techniques and heroic symbolism in favor of spontaneity and natural syntaxes" (Reynolds and McCormick 2003, 401). Their interest in the body's movement replaced preconceived notions about beauty and grace. By destroying any boundary that stood between "dance" and "not dance," "any kind of activity could be perceived as dance simply by the viewers deciding to look at it that way" (401). This dance movement was short-lived, lasting just a little over a decade. Its demise is not surprising. The dancers explored, pushed boundaries, and obliterated any preconceived notion of "dance." What they did not take into consideration was the pleasure of the audience. There simply was no sustained desire to *watch* someone sweep the floor or run in place, no matter how exquisitely done. The pleasure of the dancers was not enough to counter the lack of desire and pleasure of the spectators.

Deconstructing something, stripping it bare, removing all distinctions, and revealing its nothingness is a necessary exercise. Yet postmodern thinkers hear this critical question most: once you have exposed the artifice of everything, what do you have left? With what do you replace it? We know that our answer is that we replace it with something equally as constructed, and we set about to destroy it immediately. The Judsonites abandoned postmodern dance due to the absence of the observer's desire. Satisfied with the revelation that dance is everything, and that dance is nothing, the dancers returned to modern notions of dance. They chose to keep the thing that they destroyed, because the dance defines the dancers. If anything and everything is dance, then everyone is a dancer. If everyone is a dancer, then no one is a dancer. The joy is found in the distinction of dancer/not-dancer, in that the not-dancer desires the dancer, and in that the dancer desires the desire of the not-dancer. It is a dance.

My point is this: meaning is formed in the chasm of relationships; sometimes precise boundaries and the tensions they create are necessary for survival. Consider this example from William James (1981, 53): "The aim of a football team is not merely to get the ball to a certain goal. If that were so, they would simply get up in the middle of the night and place it there. Rather, the aim is to get it there under a set of conditions, the game's rules and other players."

We need *some* rules; we need *some* fixedness, even knowing that these things are imagined. The rules, the established structures, actually create the very conditions necessary for creativity and individual expression and for desire. Individuals, through creativity, can alter the rules but again only against the backdrop of other rules. Without the rules (i.e., some perception of an immovable object), there can be no creativity, no beauty, and no desire. This is a helpful model when we consider, for example, trans surgery. If we maintain that there is no natural or necessary relationship between gender and genitals and that gender determines sex (not the other way around), then how can one justify the need to surgically alter the body in order to conform to one's lived gender? A partial answer is that the body needs some fixedness in order to create the tensions in which beauty and desire flourish.

Yet the challenge is, how do we sustain categories so that we have a seductive, alluring tension between two seemingly fixed points *without* the violence that usually accompanies boundary preservation? Specifically, here is my question: how do we imagine gender and sex and maintain those boundaries, without the usual violence that erupts when people choose to transition, that is, do not stay within the borders of their assigned gender?[4] The goal is to find a happy medium between gender definition and gender fluidity. Surprisingly (perhaps) the Bible gives us such models.

DAVID'S DANCE

After King David and Yahweh smote the Philistines from Geba to Gezer (2 Sam 5:25), David decided to bring the ark of the covenant to Jerusalem. The ark was taken out of the house of Abinadab, and, according to 2 Sam 6:1–5, at least thirty thousand Israelites were dancing, singing, and playing every known musical instrument. In what has been interpreted as a lover's spat (Jennings 2001), David stopped the procession when he became angry with Yahweh. As the ark was jostled upon a new cart, driven by boys, pulled by oxen, downhill, Uzzah reached out to steady the ark, and Yahweh killed him.

This angered and, I would imagine, frightened David. He decided to stop and house the ark in the household of Obed-edom rather than risk the danger of bringing this terrible and capricious symbol of God's power into his new city. Once there, Obed-edom's house flourished—God poured out God's blessings seemingly because of the presence of the ark. David reassembled the nation of Israel, and, according to verse 14, David danced with all his might before the Lord, girded only with a linen ephod. In popular imagination, this garment became a vestment associated with

---

4. For current statistics regarding violence against transgendered people, see the introduction, pages 1–2.

religious ritual, due, perhaps, to the retelling of this story in 1 Chr 15:29. In that telling, David was accompanied by priests, was covered with a robe in addition to the ephod, and as Ted Jennings notes (2001, 50), the dance became "quasi-liturgical." Most notably missing from the Chronicler's account is Michal's sarcastic criticism that David had *exposed himself* to the servants' maids (a reference meaning, I think, the "lowest of the low"). Jennings suggests that the ephod would best be compared to a G-string or a jock strap—it conceals while drawing attention to that which it covers. Whatever the ephod was, Michal's comments indicate that David's dancing was uninhibited, revealing, and, in her eyes, lewd and lascivious. David, though, was without shame or regret. Indeed, he basically replies in 2 Sam 6:22, "You think that was something? You ain't seen nothin' yet."

David's dance occurs between two seemingly fixed points: a masculine Yahweh and the textually feminine people of Israel. David dances to please the Lord; he dances in celebration with the people of Israel, but mostly, David dances because he can. David dances; he moves from God to Israel and back to God. David dances, from man to woman, and back to man. God moves; Israel moves; David dances. David pauses—briefly—in the face of social judgment (as personified in Michal) and defiantly dances on.

Dancing, as I have presented it here in the Judsonite experiment and in 2 Samuel, is simultaneously a literal and a symbolic act. The dynamic bodies represent physical fluidity in general, bodies moving to, against, and through boundaries. There are points at which the bodies engage, are repelled, are embraced, yet remain in motion. As we move away from 2 Samuel, the New Testament has very little to say about dancing—and Paul specifically does not mention the word. The early Christians, especially Paul, were faced with creating a community—one distinct from the greater Roman society, particularly in attitudes about sex. As I have already pointed out, because Paul wanted to dissolve intracommunal differences by annulling food prohibitions, he relied heavily upon a closely regulated, two-gender system to reinforce the exterior community boundaries. Let me review this point here.

According to Douglas's community-building theories, the community regulates the bodies' boundaries (through food, sex, and skin laws). Paul wants to dissolve certain boundaries (those separating Jew from gentile), so he dispenses with certain laws (namely those having to do with food—and of course circumcision). However, Paul sought to strengthen the delineations between Christians and pagans, and he did this by a heightened focus on sex and gender.[5] Gender (and bodies and sex), for Paul, must be fixed, or there is no structural foundation. Dancing bodies would be highly problematic for Paul.

Jesus, on the other hand, evokes images of dancing in both canonical and noncanonical works. Though we get the supposed words of Jesus through the much later writings of the evangelists, framed and interpreted for Christians living throughout the Roman Empire forty to sixty years later, the parables (if we could pull them out of the Gospel contexts) represent what most historical Jesus scholars believe to be as close as we can get to authentic sayings of Jesus.[6] Both Matthew and Luke present an allegory of children in the agora who summon the people to dance. Both Matthew and Luke frame the material within commentary on John the Baptist. Though interpreters are divided on how Luke and Matthew understand this parable, all seem to agree that "not dancing" is an appropriate response. Here is the saying in Luke's telling:

> To what, then, can I compare the people of this generation? What are they like? They are like children sitting in the marketplace and calling out to each other: "We played the flute for you, and you did not dance; we sang a dirge, and you did not cry." (Luke 7:31–32)[7]

According to Wendy Cotter (1987), scholars who interpret this passage tend to see it one of two ways: in one interpretation, Jesus is critical of the clerical religious leaders—they are the children who are calling out, and Jesus and John do not respond appropriately to them; they expect John and Jesus to eat during the feast times, and fast during the fasting times. Instead, in this reading, John fasts during feasts, and Jesus eats during fasts. A second option, most notably held by Dieter Zeller (1977), sees the children as John and Jesus, calling to a nonresponsive people.

To be fair, determining "a meaning" for this parable seems like folly. The majority of scholars who have meticulously worked on the language, narrative structure, and rhetorical pieces of this passage claim that the

---

5. Countryman (1988), in my opinion, gives a compelling case on how, for Paul, gender concerns are central in his ecclesial formation.

6. Perhaps the most influential work here is *The Parables of Jesus* by Joachim Jeremias (1972). The Jesus Seminar, which could be considered the most suspicious critic of those words attributed to the historical Jesus, gives a higher degree of credence to parables and the aphorisms contained within.

7. Unless otherwise stated, all translations of biblical texts are my own.

pericope is "clearly composite" and "is the result of an attempt by later Christian communities to interpret the parable … which they received" (Cotter 1987, 294). One cannot assign a lone meaning to an author when the narrative is a patchwork of competing, first-century Christian ideas. Cotter does offer a compelling twist: the description of the children as seated (rather than standing) in the "marketplace" or "agora" should evoke a trial or courtroom scene (298–301). She concludes that the children are those who sit in judgment of John and Jesus; their criticism is superficial and self-righteous (302).

Still, there are problems in determining meaning from this passage. First, Jesus clearly says the children are this generation, calling out to one another. If either one of these groups (the ones calling and the ones being called) is supposed to be Jesus, he considers himself to be one of the children. In other words, the children are calling out to one another. There is not an "us against them" in this story—there is no dualism of *this* group calling out to *that* group, as interpreters paint this episode. Rather, Jesus is part of this group.

Second, there is no reason to believe that Jesus is disparaging the children. Indeed, in all other allegories involving children, Jesus sees them as the ideal, of what we should all be. For example, in Matt 19:13–14 and Mark 10:13–14, the people bring children to Jesus, and the disciples rebuke them. But Jesus says: "Hey, the children are the kingdom of heaven." While we do not know exactly what he means by this, we know that it is a good thing. In Matt 15:26–27 (Mark 7:27–28), when Jesus asserts that the bread is only for the children, he seems to see "children" as the people of Israel (of which he is, of course, one).

In general, then, it seems evident that regarding the parable of the marketplace, the symbol "children" is neither "other" (like the children of Israel) nor disparaged. Thus, any reading of this passage that sees it as dualistic, antagonistic, or divisive seems to miss the mark—though I cannot say what that mark is. Most interpretations of this passage seem to agree that it is some sort of criticism of Jesus and John—Jesus as a "glutton and drunkard" and John as demon possessed (Cotter 1987, 303). However, the key detail and one that I think is so provocative here is that Jesus's critics (as depicted in this parable and alluded to in other passages) see Jesus as the one who dances. At the very least, one could read this as Jesus's call to his people to dance—a dynamic action that, on the one hand, holds to custom, yet on the other, encourages movement across and through the conventional standards.

In modern popular imagination, it is not difficult to imagine Jesus as a dancer. The Gospels tell us he was criticized for eating and drinking too much (Matt 11:19; Luke 7:34) and that he was invited to dine often and was joyously received. A joyous reception, according to Luke 15:25, means raucous dancing. Finally, when Jesus went to a wedding feast (which one would assume involves dancing), he not only made wine, but he made *good* wine (John 2:10). To imagine a dancing Jesus is not difficult. Even the author of the apocryphal Acts of John imagines a dancing Jesus. Written in the latter part of the second century, the Acts of John tells of a Jesus who dances with his disciples at the Last Supper. In verses 94–96, the author says that Jesus assembled the disciples into a circle, instructed them to hold hands with one another, and sang a hymn as he danced within the circle and they danced around him. Apart from this reference, there is no indication that this happened with the historical Jesus—but what it does tell us is that at least one Christian community included dance as part of the eucharistic ritual, a central ritual that sought to erase distinctions among Christians, to dissolve the divisions between body and spirit, and possibly for Paul, in its rudimentary existence, to remove the division between Jews and gentiles.

Table fellowship (as, perhaps, a precursor to a eucharistic ritual) seemed to be a central symbol for Paul as a visible sign that "there is neither Jew nor Greek" (Gal 3:28).[8] Faced, on the one hand, with the potential rift in his communities between gentiles and Jews and, on the other hand, the rift between Christ followers and the rest of the citizens of the empire, the negotiation of food (of who eats what and with whom) was paramount. If one returns again to the work of Douglas, it should be no surprise that Paul relies so heavily on food. A community's boundaries are built and maintained through its purity concerns, which center on food. A community—every community—is built upon the laws that police a body's boundaries. Food sanctions and prohibitions are the most stable and most visible of these codes. And the keyword here, for Paul, is *stability*.

Paul has no use for dancing bodies. Paul needs bodies to be static and inflexible in order to rest his ἐκκλησία upon a rock—and that rock for Paul is gender stability. Therefore, he reifies gender differences and renders them "natural." Jesus, on the other hand, was up to something else.

---

8. See Laura Nasrallah (2014) for an insightful article on Paul's commentary on food and meals; she suggests that the practice of eating together was central to Paul's ethical program; see also Ringe 1986; Sandelin 2002; and Yeung 2011.

Jesus was bringing about the kingdom of God. Jesus sought to dissolve the chasm between humanity and the love of God, of God's own presence in this world. Like David, Jesus danced in the lacuna between heaven and earth to make the two as one.

Though Paul wants to bring his community to God, it is a secondary concern, which he brings about through his understanding of the body of Christ: a static, unchanging body of Christ—a gendered body with fixed boundaries. Paul seeks to reinforce, not dissolve, the structures that are grounded in supposed "natural" gender binaries. King David shows us that to approach God, to attempt to dissolve into God, we must dance. The apostle Paul does not call us out to dance. But Jesus does.

The erroneous presumption of gender and sexual stability is hurtful; the consequences for those who know this and practice this in their daily lives are severe. Indeed, we punish those who fail to do their gender correctly. We kill those who seek to change it, those who transition.

What I have offered here is a possible and alternative model, based on the sayings and traditions of Jesus, that allows movement and dynamism to be the foundation of how we understand the human condition and the manifestation of the sacred within that condition. Butler tells us that, for our gender to be deemed as "normal," we must fit into a predetermined set of qualities. Yet having the limits of our "truths" circumscribed in advance, she asks a poignant question: "Who can I become in such a world where the meaning and limits of the subject are set out in advance?" (2006, 184). Then she states a sad reality of many people: "What happens when I begin to become that for which there is no place in the given regime of truth?" (184). When Paul states in Gal 3 that there is no male or female in Christ Jesus, maybe he was on to something. Though Paul himself never substantiates this claim for his own community, perhaps we can grab hold of the essence of some of Jesus's teachings that eluded Paul—that in the paradigm of dancing, of dynamic movement, we let go of the unyielding categories of gender that confine us and keep us apart from Jesus's idea of the kingdom of God, yet hold on to some of the tensions, borne from moving between a degree of an imagined fixedness of physical bodies, that make desire and beauty possible.

5

SLENDER MAN AND THE NEW HORRORS
OF THE APOCALYPSE

Teresa J. Hornsby

We live in a fantasy. We deny that the world is chaotic; we think that the world fits into neat categories; we believe that there is an "order of things." At the foundation of all order, of all neatness and compartmentalization, is the fiction of a gender binary. We have deluded ourselves into accepting that gender is static and fits neatly into an either/or of male/female. This gender binary is what holds the rest of the world together: capitalism can only exist if some bodies are worth less than other bodies; Western religious institutions prevail only if there is imperfection longing for perfection; medical and mental institutions need the sick; and so on. All of these "lesser" elements of any binary relationship are feminized.[1] But the world is not neat and tidy. Things do not fit into two defined units. Things get messy, ambiguous; there is blood, decay; we suffer, and we die. In this volume, we have endeavored to deconstruct one small part of this reiteration of the gender binary by rereading paradigmatic biblical texts through a "trans gaze." Yet, as this present work unfolds and ends, there are still some unanswered questions: Why are the rates of violence against trans bodies so extraordinarily high? In what ways can our trans hermeneutic pragmatically address these crises?

---

1. Following Foucault's thesis (1978) that power is produced and maintained via social institutions, subsequent work makes clear that integral to each institution's existence is a hierarchized gender binary. For economic theory, see Hennessy 2000; for the gendering of religious ideologies, see Althaus-Reid 2000; for the feminization of illnesses, see Lorber and Moore 2002; and Chesler 1972.

Historically, we of Eurocentric heritage target those things that embody ambiguity. It is how and why we create our "monsters."[2] One manifestation of this fear is the extraordinarily high levels of violence enacted upon trans bodies; they are expressions of a collective terror of ambiguity. Yet there are new constructions of horror, horror that is produced in a new and present apocalyptic crisis, and these horrors show signs of hope: the font from which the terror flows is no longer ambiguity but a more tangible (or "real") threat.

Slender Man lurks. Freakishly tall, clad in a black and white business suit, white, bald, and faceless, he preys on the innocent. Slender Man is the monster of this new, as yet unnamed, generation. He inherits the facelessness of Jason (the *Halloween* series) and the ethereal nature of Freddie (*Nightmare on Elm Street*), but his birth and construction are a phenomenon in the art of narratival monster building called "open sourcing." Slender Man started simply in 2009 as a few photographs submitted to an online forum called "Something Awful"; the group invited users to submit an image of pure horror. A participant who called himself "Victor Surge" uploaded photoshopped pictures of children playing in a schoolyard with a mysterious figure lurking in the shadows behind; the next photo showed them running toward the camera, their faces betraying sheer terror. In her article "Open-Sourcing Horror," Shira Chess writes,

> On 10 June, the tenor of the forum shifted dramatically, though, when a user posted two "photos" and a news story identifying a faceless **"Slender Man"** in a suit who stalked children. Almost immediately, an obsessive interest in the **Slender Man** took over the forum discussions. Near constant additions were added to the **Slender Man** mythos with new photographs, drawings, short fiction, and even wood cuttings showing his appearance in different times and places. (2012, 375)

From these fragmented beginnings, Slender Man has become a paranormal terror that exists in the shadows, stalks small children, often appearing in their dreams before they disappear. His origins are ambiguous; his identity shifts; he is faceless and nameless. His construction has been the result of thousands of online users creating fake documentary footage, photos, games, news items, blog entries, and more. The primary locus of this construction is an online series called *Marble Hornets*, the story of a

---

2. See Guest's discussion of Shildrick's *Embodying the Monster* (2002) in ch. 2 above.

film student named Alex who is shooting a film in the summer of 2009. As the series progresses, Alex becomes paranoid, irritable, and abruptly stops filming. He claims that the working conditions have become impossible and threatens to burn all of the videos. Alex disappears, and a friend decides to go through each film to determine the cause of Alex's deteriorating mental state. Each of the videos makes up the 135 episodes of *Marble Hornets*.

Though its origins are humble, the introduction and the first Slender Man entry on the *Marble Hornets* YouTube channel have over 12.3 million views.[3] Other videos (a fake documentary, a short film, pseudo news reports, police recordings, etc.) have millions of views for each site.[4] The open-sourced construction from which the Slender Man ascended is a phenomenon in itself: thousands take part in the creation, millions watch. The mythos of the Slender Man began with eerie, fake, "eyewitness" photographic accounts, such as this entry by Surge: "'We didn't want to go, we didn't want to kill them, but its persistent silence and outstretched arms horrified and comforted us at the same time…'—1983, photographer unknown, assumed dead" (Chess 2012, 378).

Horrific indeed. The *Marble Hornets* videos are chilling, eerily unsettling, but at the same time enticing. What is it that draws *millions* to such a simple tale? Being "horrified and comforted" is exactly the reaction that Julia Kristeva observes in each encounter with the abject—the point at which "the real" dissolves the fictions that we have created to contain it.[5] The abject is that which cannot be subsumed into order; it cannot be categorized or managed in service to structure and security. The abject erupts at the borders—the areas that cannot be defined, contained, or restrained.

> It is death infecting life. Abject. It is something rejected from which one does not part, from which one does not protect oneself as from an object. Imaginary uncanniness and real threat, it beckons to us and ends up engulfing us…. It is … what disturbs identity, system, order. What does not respect borders, positions, rules. (Kristeva 1982, 4)

> It lies there, quite close, but it cannot be assimilated. It beseeches, worries, and fascinates desire, which, nevertheless, does not let itself be seduced. Apprehensive, desire turns aside; sickened, it rejects. (1)

---

3. See Marble Hornets 2009. "Entry # 1" presently has over five million views.

4. See J. Jones 2013. This short film presently has over seven million views. Also see fxscreamer 2010. This short film presently has well over seven million views.

5. For a discussion of Kristeva's "Abject," see page 22.

The tales of the Slender Man, I think, represent the anxieties of the abject as they emerge through the genre of open-sourced horror; this is the type of fiction that can do justice to the terror that erupts when the abject threatens the flimsily produced edifice of safety and security: the source is ethereal; there is no static substance; and its signification is open and dynamic. The Slender Man and its productive apparatus stand in the place of a gaping void—a תהום onto which we place our present anxieties.[6] This תהום, the void that we encounter in Genesis and upon which we are perched precariously, simultaneously drawn in and repelled by the irresistible vertigo of staring into the chasm, expresses the abject, the chaotic uncertainty that comes with the growing realization that there is no ground of being, that there is only instability, and that this instability and uncertainty have always been part of creation. Yet the distinction is that these anxieties, laid bare in creation, are now projected into the future; the relatively new genre of open sourcing functions in part as a postmodern apocalypse.

The cultural processes of open sourcing, especially as it intersects with the genre of horror, allow us to examine, clearly and concisely, how and why we construct our monsters. Open sourcing took off in the 1990s, following the free software movement of the 1980s (Chess 2012, 381). The distinctions of creating fiction in this way are that the processes are open to anonymous collaboration; it is dynamic, which means that while it maintains certain core pieces (e.g., the freakish height and dark suit of Slender Man), the constructions are fluid. It remains without definition, as it is modifiable in infinite ways. While open sourcing may not seem that distinct from the constructions of fictions in general, that these productions are done online, with unfamiliar collaborators, and with little to no hard-and-fast rules in place provides insight into the ways in which the creation of monsters parallels cultural anxieties and attends to social needs.

Horror, according to Kristeva, is the privileged signifier of the thing that terrifies us most, the abject. The abject appears when the realities of our own mortality (decay, disease, death) seep through the order that we have constructed for ourselves. Those anxieties and fears that erupt can only be expressed through horror, the "ultimate coding of our crises" (1982, 208). Confrontations with the abject terrorize us, because they lay bare the ambiguities, thus the instabilities, upon which we place everything. Horror, as Kristeva explains, is when we are confronted with an

---

6. For a discussion of תהום, see pages 23–25.

ambiguity that will not allow us to deny the reality of death. "Abjection is above all ambiguity. Because, while releasing a hold, it does not radically cut off the subject from what threatens it—on the contrary, *abjection acknowledges it to be in perpetual danger*" (9, emphasis added).

In the Christian canon, these horrors tend to be expressed through the genre of the apocalypse. The mythos of the Slender Man is not of the genre of apocalyptic literature per se,[7] but it is produced in an atmosphere that exhibits the same anxieties as those that have historically produced an apocalypse. The apocalypse typically addresses some imminent crisis and "evokes the reign of chaos, which renders meaningless concepts such as justice and goodness" (Carey 2005, 228). An apocalypse is an intertwined matrix of two purposes: to describe the social situation at hand and to suggest a strategy that would relieve the stresses of present evil (Collins 1987, 32). Apocalypses

> revealed not only the future course of history, or the final disposition of mortals, they also unveiled—that is, interpreted—present reality. Monsters characterize imperial brutality; cosmic portents reflect social injustice; heavenly glories display the rule of the transcendent over the ordinary. (Carey 2005, 228)

In other words, our horrors reenact the confusion that we experience when nothing makes sense: What is "right"? To what are we tethered? Who or what demands and enforces justice? Chaos. No stability.

---

7. The characteristics of the apocalypse are as follows: it is grim and dark (Novak 2012, 531); it usually portrays a venerable human guided by a supernatural force (depended upon for interpretation [Collins 1987, 5–6]); it is an "elaborate review of history, presented in the form of a prophecy and culminating in a time of crisis and eschatological upheaval" (6). It is a final judgment, with a destruction of the wicked and a hortatory aspect (6). "The world is mysterious and revelation must be transmitted from a supernatural source, through the mediation of angels; there is a hidden world of angels and demons that is directly relevant to human destiny; and this destiny is finally determined by a definitive eschatological judgment. In short, human life is bounded in the present by the supernatural world of angels and demons and in the future by the inevitability of a final judgment" (8). Greg Carey lists the following four characteristics (following Collins): "the expectation of a final judgment, in which God separates sinners from the righteous; hope for resurrection of the righteous dead to a glorious realm; reflection upon God's role in history, both past and future, leading to a new age of justice and deliverance; and speculation concerning a heavenly messianic figure—a Son of Man, Elect One, Righteous One, or Messiah—who will administer final justice upon the world" (2005, 19).

Here is the essence of our present, postmodern horror: our "realities" are contingent upon a dualistic paradigm, and that paradigm depends upon a two- (and only two) gender system; it is upon that dualism that *all* order stands. To break the imaginary two-gender paradigm is to destroy the foundation of all order. In other words, all comfort, security, order, logic, sense—all rest upon ... nothing.

Thus the "monsters" are those things that we imagine to threaten that stability; they are the entities that do not fit neatly into a binary—the zombie, the vampire, Frankenstein's monster (neither alive nor dead), the werewolf (neither human nor nonhuman animal). In our current state of hyperbinaryism, the trans person's body has become ambiguity personified. The trans person, whom Julia Serano names "a whipping girl," has become a target for all woes and is often portrayed as monstrous; thus, in our present apocalyptic crisis, the trans person is perceived as deserving the extraordinarily high rates of violence. I think this is due to the fact that a trans person is a flesh-and-blood, incontrovertible proof that a stable and naturally created gender binary is imaginary; the trans body is the ambiguity that remains connected to the subject, that is, the abject that cannot be subsumed into the imaginary. However, the abject, or the "monstrous," is not (as Kristeva tends to imply) something that is apart from a carefully constructed worldview, but should be viewed, as Judith Butler and Margrit Shildrick have argued, as part of the constructed order. Abjection, chaos, the monstrous, ambiguity—whatever the term—is an essential element of a joyous existence. Yet the hierarchical, imaginary dualism upon which Western civilization stands renders those realities (abjections) as demonic, horrific, and dangerous.

If we could read biblical texts without the assumptions brought on by a gender binary, we would read the canonical Apocalypse with all of its abjection, fluidity, seepage, and transitions intact. That the Christian canon concludes with what could arguably be the most liminally abjective, queer writing in the entire Bible confirms, for me, that we are heading in the right direction when we recognize the dynamism of the text and its refusal to be subsumed into hierarchical dualism.

Tina Pippin is one scholar who has already recognized the possibilities of a trans hermeneutical reading of Revelation. She remarks that in John's Apocalypse, "nothing is stable ..., especially gender and desire" (2006, 72). Pippin observes that 144,000 males become the bride of Christ (69), and "by becoming women, men can love a man (God) without the threat of homosexuality" (71). Thus the canonical Apocalypse cannot function without transvestitism and homoeroticism as its central tropes. Actually, one should expect the canon to conclude in this way, especially if we take into account that Jesus is a site where so many dualisms are dissolved. Jesus's ambiguity exists usually not as a result of any one portrayal of him, but as a result of how the reader imagines Jesus after combining all the evangelists' portraits. Mark's human Jesus exists simultaneously with John's ethereal Logos. Theologian Robert Goss reflects upon the "Queer Fluidity" in his commentary on John's Gospel:

> John's Gospel develops the most profound Christological reflections upon Jesus that we encounter in the Christian canon of scriptures.... It weaves the gender fluidity of Jesus as the embodiment of Divine Wisdom with Jesus as God's revelation. Jesus is the supreme manifestation of God's Word and embodiment of Divine Wisdom. It expresses an alternative to the male imagery of God. (2006, 550)

Goss goes on to quote Martin Scott:

> The point of John's Wisdom Christology is precisely that Jesus Sophia is not mere man, but rather the incarnation of both the male and the female expression of the divine, albeit within the limitation of human flesh. (Scott 1992, 72)

In addition to a fluidity of gender, Jesus's body becomes the site where multiple dualisms collapse: divinity and humanity merge; "this world" blends into "other world"; and through the resurrection, physicality and ethereality are one. It is no exaggeration to say that all things *trans* lie at the heart of Christian belief: the *trans*formation of the resurrected corpse; the *trans*ubstantiation of bread to body, of wine to blood; and of course, the *trans*ition of God to human to God. John's Apocalypse, then, holds a representation of Jesus as a site of what Laura Jane Grace (a trans front woman for the punk group Against Me!) calls "the true trans." Jesus is a "true trans" in that as he appears in this apocalypse, dichotomies are collapsed: physical/spiritual, human/divine, male/female, I/other, human/animal, alive/dead, and so on. He exists in the interstices of any imagined order; he becomes a personification of the abject body. Thus a trans hermeneutic of the Apocalypse recognizes that one cannot do justice to the final book of the canon unless the apocalyptic Jesus and his court of transvestite brides are accepted as the queer and chaotic beings they are. However, I must be clear here: the Christian Apocalypse is basically a trans-phobic expression as it conveys a debilitating fear of ambiguity and fluidity. Ironically, as Pippin notes, its mode for articulating those fears is through trans bodies and ambiguous sexualities; yet the phobias are never resolved, and in the violent end, the dualistic and hierarchical constructs are left in place.

Likewise, the apocalyptically produced tale of the Slender Man betrays our collective fear of chaos and anxieties that originate with ambiguity and the failures of a system that hopelessly tries to stabilize them. What is striking about the Slender Man is the site upon which all fear is placed: a tall, white, faceless male in a business suit who comes after our children; to quote Pippin (1999, 79), "the evil powers are in plain view now."

As my students and I discussed the Slender Man, we pondered the question, what is scary about a white, aging man in a business suit? Our conversations turned to horrifically "real" evils brought about by "men in business suits." We talked about Wall Street, rampant corporate greed that has led to human trafficking, the destruction of natural resources, the colonization of indigenous people—in other words, a neoliberal capital-ist ideology that is sustained by a gender binary that creates expendable bodies. A gender binary renders some bodies less valuable than other bodies, which creates cheap labor, which produces profit (see Hornsby 2011).

The promise that modernity, neoliberal capitalism, and Fordism would guarantee a safe and secure world is empty. The symbol of twenty-first-century colonial power (white, male, capitalist) has become the monster that haunts our waking life and threatens the lives of our children. Simply put: the Slender Man is a personification of a neoliberal, capitalist evil.

The second-century horror, John's Revelation, expresses—violently, grotesquely—the very real terror of that time and that place: a dissolution of boundaries and their subsumption into an evil system (Pippin 2006, 72). These fears are personified in the image of demonic and feminized sexual-ity, the whore of Babylon. Their resolution is found, partly, in ambiguous sexuality and trans bodies, that is, a seepage of the abject into the fantasy; yet this horror ends in genocide. The twenty-first-century horror, the Slen-der Man, betrays the same anxieties (fear of ambiguity, fear of the abject, and fear of the dissolution of the subject), yet there is something new here. The site from which all terror originates in this tale is, indeed, a very "real" monster. It is a monster that exists among us, has sponsored genocide, the destruction of whole civilizations, and the enslavement of millions. Though this horror is still in process, there is hope here. Though the anxieties may have emerged from abjective concerns (it is the programmed ideology after all), the significance of the fact that this horror is transitive and multivocatively produced cannot be overstated. Open-sourced horror, in this case, becomes an expression of the abject; it is the means by which the abject is given representation and subjectivity. More, the "monster," the Slender Man, reveals the logical end, the "real" consequences of accepting an imaginary and dualistic order and *not* embracing ambiguity, discursiveness, and bodies in transition. The canonical Apocalypse is a failed and hopeless vision that ends in death. But this new apocalyptic response, one that embraces ambiguity, a trans hermeneutic if you will, knows the "real" threat that brings our end—a neoliberal capitalism born of greed; and this hermeneutic imparts a means of survival: to embrace the ambiguous and purge the illusion of a gender binary. No more binary, no more monsters.

Bibliography

Ackerman, Susan. 1998. *Warrior, Dancer, Seductress, Queen: Women in Judges and Biblical Israel*. New York: Doubleday.

Allen, Mariette Pathy. 2010. "Connecting Body and Mind: How Transgender People Changed Their Self-Image." *Women and Performance: A Journal of Feminist Theory* 20:267–83.

Althaus-Reid, Marcella. 2000. *Indecent Theology: Theological Perversions in Sex, Gender and Politics*. London: Routledge.

———. 2003. *The Queer God*. London: Routledge.

Appler, Deborah. 2006. "Jezebel." *NIDB* 3:313–14.

Apter, Emily. 1998. "Reflections on Gynophobia." Pages 102–22 in *Coming out of Feminism?* Edited by Mandy Merck, Naomi Segal, and Elizabeth Wright. Oxford: Blackwell.

Barr, James. 1999. "One Man, or All Humanity?" Pages 3–21 in *Recycling Biblical Figures: Papers Read at a NOSTER Colloquium in Amsterdam 12–13 May 1997*. Edited by Athalya Brenner and J. W. van Henton. Leiderdorp: Deo.

Beauvoir, Simone de. 1972. *The Second Sex*. Translated and edited by H. M. Parshley. Harmondsworth: Penguin.

Bergman, J., W. von Soden, and P. R. Ackroyd. 1986. "יָד." *TDOT* 5: 393–426.

Bindel, Julie. 2004. "Gender Benders, Beware." *The Guardian*. http://tinyurl.com/SBL0686a.

Boer, Roland. 2012. *The Earthy Nature of the Bible: Fleshly Readings of Sex, Masculinity, and Carnality*. Basingstoke: Palgrave Macmillan.

Boler, Megan. 1997. "The Risks of Empathy." *Cultural Studies* 11:253–73.

Bornstein, Kate. 1994. *Gender Outlaw: On Men, Women and the Rest of Us*. New York: Routledge.

———. 1998. *My Gender Workbook: How to Become a Real Man, a Real Woman, the Real You, or Something Else Entirely*. New York: Routledge.

————. 2006. "Gender Terror, Gender Rage." Pages 236–43 in *The Transgender Studies Reader*. Edited by Susan Stryker and Stephen Whittle. New York: Routledge.

Brenner, Athalya. 1997. *The Intercourse of Knowledge: On Gendering Desire and "Sexuality" in the Hebrew Bible*. BibInt 26. Leiden: Brill.

Brooten, Bernadette J. 1996. *Love between Women: Early Christian Responses to Female Homoeroticism*. Chicago: University of Chicago Press.

Brueggemann, Walter. 2000. *1 and 2 Kings*. SHBC. Macon, GA: Smyth & Helwys.

Burkett, Elinor. 2015. "What Makes a Woman?" *New York Times*. http://tinyurl.com/SBL0686c.

Butler, Judith. 1988. "Performative Acts and Gender Constitution: An Essay in Phenomenology and Feminist Theory." *Theatre Journal* 40:519–31.

————. 1990. *Gender Trouble: Feminism and the Subversion of Identity*. New York: Routledge.

————. 1993. *Bodies That Matter: On the Discursive Limits of "Sex."* New York: Routledge.

————. 2004. *Undoing Gender*. New York: Routledge.

————. 2006. "Doing Justice to Someone: Sex Reassignment and Allegories of Transsexuality." Pages 183–93 in *The Transgender Studies Reader*. Edited by Susan Stryker and Stephen Whittle. New York: Routledge.

Camp, Claudia. 1992. "1 and 2 Kings." Pages 96–109 in *The Women's Bible Commentary*. Edited by Carol A. Newsom and Sharon H. Ringe. London: SPCK.

Carden, Michael. 2006. "Genesis/Bereshit." Pages 21–60 in *The Queer Bible Commentary*. Edited by Deryn Guest, Bob Goss, Mona West, and Tom Bohache. London: SCM.

Carey, Greg. 2005. *Ultimate Things: An Introduction to Jewish and Christian Apocalyptic Literature*. St. Louis: Chalice.

Chapman, Cynthia R. 2004. *The Gendered Language of Warfare in the Israelite-Assyrian Encounter*. HSM 62. Winona Lake, IN: Eisenbrauns.

Chesler, Phyllis. 1972. *Women and Madness*. New York: Doubleday.

Chess, Shira. 2012. "Open-Sourcing Horror: The Slender Man, *Marble Hornets,* and Genre Negotiation." *Information, Communication, and Society* 15:374–93.

Children's Bible in Colour. 1964. London: Hamlyn.

Christian Institute. 2002. "Transsexualism: Mind over Matter." The Christian Institute. http://tinyurl.com/SBL0686d.

Clines, David J. A. 1995. "David the Man: The Construction of Masculinity in the Hebrew Bible." Pages 212–43 in *Interested Parties: The Ideology of Writers and Readers of the Hebrew Bible*. Edited by David J. A. Clines. JSOTSup 205. GCT 1. Sheffield: Sheffield Academic.

———. 2002. "He-Prophets: Masculinity as a Problem for the Hebrew Prophets and Their Interpreters." Pages 311–27 in *Sense and Sensitivity: Essays on Reading the Bible in Memory of Robert Carroll*. Edited by Alastair G. Hunter and Philip R. Davies. LHBOTS 348. Sheffield: Sheffield Academic.

———. 2003. "אדם, the Hebrew for 'Human, Humanity': A Response to James Barr." *VT* 53:297–310.

———. 2010. "Dancing and Shining at Sinai: Playing the Man in Exodus." Pages 54–63 in *Men and Masculinity in the Hebrew Bible and Beyond*. Edited by Ovidiu Creangă. BMW 33. Sheffield: Sheffield Phoenix.

Cogan, Mordechai, and Hayim Tadmor. 1988. *II Kings: A New Translation with Introduction and Commentary*. AB 11. New York: Doubleday.

Cohn, Robert L. 2000. *2 Kings*. Berit Olam. Collegeville, MN: Liturgical Press.

Collins, John J. 1987. *The Apocalyptic Imagination: An Introduction to the Jewish Matrix of Christianity*. New York: Crossroad.

Cotter, Wendy J. 1987. "The Parable of the Children in the Marketplace, Q (Lk.) 7:31–35: An Examination of the Parable's Image and Significance." *NovT* 29:289–304.

Countryman, L. William. 1988. *Dirt, Greed, and Sex: Sexual Ethics in the New Testament and Their Implications for Today*. Philadelphia: Fortress.

Creangă, Ovidiu, ed. 2010. *Men and Masculinity in the Hebrew Bible and Beyond*. BMW 33. Sheffield: Sheffield Phoenix.

Cromwell, Jason. 1999. *Transmen and FTMs: Identities, Bodies, Genders, and Sexualities*. Urbana, IL: University of Illinois Press.

Daly, Mary. 1978. *Gyn/Ecology: The Metaethics of Radical Feminism*. London: Women's Press.

Day, John. 1985. *God's Conflict with the Dragon and the Sea: Echoes of a Canaanite Myth in the Old Testament*. UCOP 35. Cambridge: Cambridge University Press.

Day, Peggy L. 1992. "Anat: Ugarit's 'Mistress of Animals.'" *JNES* 51:181–90.

Delcor, M. 1967. "Two Special Meanings of the word יד in Biblical Hebrew." *JSS* 12:230–40.

Dever, William G. 2005. *Did God Have a Wife? Archaeology and Folk Religion in Ancient Israel*. Grand Rapids: Eerdmans.

DiPalma, Brian Charles. 2010. "De/Constructing Masculinity in Exodus 1–4." Pages 36–53 in *Men and Masculinity in the Hebrew Bible and Beyond*. Edited by Ovidiu Creangă. BMW 33. Sheffield: Sheffield Phoenix.

Doty, Alexander. 1993. *Making Things Perfectly Queer: Interpreting Mass Culture*. Minneapolis: University of Minnesota Press.

Douglas, Mary. 1966. *Purity and Danger: An Analysis of the Concepts of Purity and Taboo*. London: Routledge.

Dunbar, James. 2006. "Race, Gender, and Sexual Orientation in Hate Crime Victimization: Identity Politics or Identity Risk?" *Violence and Victims* 21:323–37.

Ellul, Jacques. 1972. *The Politics of God and the Politics of Man*. Translated and edited by Geoffrey W. Bromiley. Grand Rapids: Eerdmans.

Enke, Anne Finn. 2012. "Introduction." Pages 1–15 in *Transfeminist Perspectives in and beyond Transgender and Gender Studies*. Edited by Anne Finn Enke. Philadelphia: Temple University Press.

Evangelical Alliance Policy Commission. 2000. *Transsexuality*. Carlisle: Paternoster.

Feinberg, Leslie. 1993. *Stone Butch Blues: A Novel*. Los Angeles: Alyson.

———. 2006. "Transgender Liberation: A Movement Whose Time Has Come." Pages 205–20 in *The Transgender Studies Reader*. Edited by Susan Stryker and Stephen Whittle. New York: Routledge.

Fewell, Danna Nolan, and David M. Gunn. 1993. *Gender, Power, and Promise: The Subject of the Bible's First Story*. Nashville: Abingdon.

Foucault, Michel. 1978. *An Introduction*. Vol. 1 of *A History of Sexuality*. Translated by Robert Hurley. New York: Pantheon.

Frye, Northrop. 1982. *The Great Code: The Bible and Literature*. London: Routledge.

fxscreamer. 2010. "Slender Suits: The Documentary of Slender Man." YouTube. http://tinyurl.com/SBL0686p.

Gagné, Patricia, and Richard Tewksbury. 1998. "Conformity Pressures and Gender Resistance among Transgendered Individuals." *Social Problems* 45:81–101.

Gaines, Janet. 1999. *Music in the Old Bones: Jezebel through the Ages*. Carbondal, IL: Southern Illinois University Press.

García-Treto, Francisco O. 1992. "The Fall of the House: A Carnivalesque Reading of 2 Kings 9 and 10." Pages 153–71 in *Reading between Texts: Intertextuality and the Hebrew Bible*. Edited by Danna Nolan Fewell. Louisville: Westminster John Knox.

Gilmore, David D. 1990. *Manhood in the Making: Cultural Concepts of Masculinity*. New Haven: Yale University Press.

———. 1996. "Above and Below: Toward a Social Geometry of Gender." *American Anthropologist* 98:54–66.

Golden, Carla R. 2000. "Still Seeing Differently, After All These Years." *Feminism and Psychology* 10:30–35.

Görg, M. 2006. "תֹהוּ." *TDOT* 15: 565–74.

Goss, Robert E. 2006. "John." Pages 548–65 in *The Queer Bible Commentary*. Edited by Deryn Guest, Robert E. Goss, Mona West, and Thomas Bohache. London: SCM.

Gray, John. 1977. *1 and 2 Kings: A Commentary*. 3rd rev. ed. OTL. London: SCM.

Greengard, Samuel. 2012. "Guide to Knee Replacement Implants and Their Manufacturers." healthline. http://tinyurl.com/SBL0686h.

Greer, Germaine. 1999. *The Whole Woman*. London: Doubleday.

Gunkel, Hermann. 1895. *Schöpfung und Chaos in Urzeit und Endzeit: Eine Religionsgeschichtliche Untersuchung über Gen 1 und Ap Joh 12*. Göttingen: Vandenhoeck & Ruprecht.

Haddox, Susan E. 2010. "Favored Sons and Subordinate Masculinities." Pages 2–10 in *Men and Masculinity in the Hebrew Bible and Beyond*. Edited by Ovidiu Creangă. BMW 33. Sheffield: Sheffield Phoenix.

Hadley, Judith M. 2000. *The Cult of Asherah in Ancient Israel and Judah: Evidence for a Hebrew Goddess*. UCOP 57. Cambridge: Cambridge University Press.

Halberstam, Jack. 2012. "On Pronouns." Personal website. http://tinyurl.com/SBL0686j.

Halberstam, Judith. 1998. *Female Masculinity*. Durham, NC: Duke University Press.

———. 2001. "The Transgender Gaze in Boys Don't Cry." *Screen* 42:294–98.

Hale, C. Jacob. 1998. "Consuming the Living, Disremembering the Dead in the Butch/FTM Borderlands." *GLQ* 4:311–48.

Hamelynck, Karel. 2010. "The Story of Knee Replacement." Paper presented at the Orthopedic Workshop and Conference, Hospital of the Merciful Sisters. Linz, Austria, 20 November 2010.

Hamilton, Victor P. 1990. *The Book of Genesis: Chapters 1–17*. NICOT. Grand Rapids: Eerdmans.

Hasel, Gerhard F. 1972. "The Significance of the Cosmology in Genesis 1 in Relation to Ancient Near Eastern Parallels." *AUSS* 10:1–20.

Hausman, Bernice L. 2001. "Recent Transgender Theory." *Feminist Studies* 27:465–90.

Hennegan, Alison. 1988. "On Becoming a Lesbian Reader." Pages 165–90 in *Sweet Dreams: Sexuality, Gender and Popular Fiction.* Edited by Susannah Radstone. London: Lawrence & Wishart.

Hennessy, Rosemary. 2000. *Profit and Pleasure: Sexual Identities in Late Capitalism.* New York: Routledge.

Hens-Piazza, Gina. 2006. *1–2 Kings.* AOTC. Nashville: Abingdon.

Heyes, Cressida J. 2003. "Feminist Solidarity after Queer Theory: The Case of Transgender." *Signs* 28:1093–1120.

Hill, Darryl B. 2002. "Genderism, Transphobia, and Gender Bashing: A Framework for Interpreting Anti-transgender Violence." Pages 113–36 in *Understanding and Dealing with Violence: A Multicultural Approach.* Edited by Barbara C. Wallace and Robert T. Carter. Thousand Oaks, CA: Sage.

Hill, Darryl B., and Brian L. B. Willoughby. 2005. "The Development and Validation of the Genderism and Transphobia Scale." *Sex Roles* 53:531–44.

Hillers, Delbert. 1973. "The Bow of Aqhat: The Meaning of a Mythological Theme." Pages 71–80 in *Orient and Occident: Essays Presented to Cyrus H. Gordon on the Occasion of His 65th Birthday.* Edited by Harry A. Hoffner. AOAT 22. Kevelaer: Butzon & Bercker; Neukirchen-Vluyn: Neukirchener Verlag.

Hines, Sally. 2006. "What's the Difference? Bringing Particularity to Queer Studies of Transgender." *Journal of Gender Studies* 15:49–66.

Hoffner, Harry A., Jr. 1966. "Symbols for Masculinity and Femininity: Their Use in Ancient Near Eastern Sympathetic Magic Rituals." *JBL* 85:326–34.

Hollibaugh, Amber, and Cherríe Moraga. 1983. "What We're Rollin around in Bed with: Sexual Silences in Feminism." Pages 404–17 in *Powers of Desire: The Politics of Sexuality.* Edited by Ann Snitow, Christine Stansell, and Sharon Thompson. London: Virago.

"Homosexuality and Biblical Interpretation." n.d. Conservapedia. http://tinyurl.com/SBL0686i.

Hornsby, Teresa J. 2011. "Capitalism, Masochism, and Biblical Interpretation." Pages 137–56 in *Bible Trouble: Queer Reading at the Boundaries of Biblical Scholarship.* Edited by Teresa J. Hornsby and Ken Stone. SemeiaSt 67. Atlanta: Society of Biblical Literature

———. 2014. "The Dance of Gender: David, Jesus and Paul." *Neot* 48:75–91.

House of Bishops. 2003. *Some Issues in Human Sexuality: A Guide to the Debate*. London: Church House.

Huskey, Melynda. 2002. "Queering the Picture Book." *The Lion and the Unicorn* 26:66–77.

Innes, Sherrie A., and Michele E. Lloyd. 1996. "G. I. Joes in Barbie Land: Recontexualizing Butch in Twentieth-Century Lesbian Culture." Pages 9–34 in *Queer Studies: A Lesbian, Gay, Bisexual, and Transgender Anthology*. Edited by Brett Beemyn and Mickey Eliason. New York: New York University Press.

James, William. 1981. *Pragmatism*. Indianapolis: Hackett.

Jeffreys, Sheila. 2003. *Unpacking Queer Politics: A Lesbian Feminist Perspective*. Cambridge: Polity.

———. 2005. *Beauty and Misogyny: Harmful Cultural Practices in the West*. London: Routledge.

Jennings, Theodore W., Jr. 2001. "YHWH as Erastes." Pages 36–74 in *Queer Commentary and the Hebrew Bible*. Edited by Ken Stone. LHBOTS 334. Sheffield: Sheffield Academic.

Jeremias, Joachim. 1972. *The Parables of Jesus*. 2nd ed. New York: Scribner's Sons.

Jones, G. H. 1984. *1 and 2 Kings*. NCBC. Grand Rapids: Eerdmans.

Jones, Justin, dir. 2013. *Fathom: Slender Man Short Film*. Gearmark.TV. http://tinyurl.com/SBL0686n.

Kander, Jessica. 2011. "Reading Queer Subtexts in Children's Literature." MA thesis. Eastern Michigan University.

Koehler, Ludwig, Walter Baumgartner, and Johann Jakob Stamm. 1994–1999. *The Hebrew and Aramaic Lexicon of the Old Testament*. Translated and edited under the supervision of M. E. J. Richardson. 5 vols. Leiden: Brill.

Kolakowski, Victoria S. 1997a. "The Concubine and the Eunuch: Queering up the Breeder's Bible." Pages 35–49 in *Our Families, Our Values: Snapshots of Queer Kinship*. Edited by Robert E. Goss and Amy Adams Squire Strongheart. Binghamton, NY: Harrington Park.

———. 1997b. "Towards a Christian Ethical Response to Transsexual Persons." *Theology and Sexuality* 6:10–31.

———. 2000. "Throwing a Party: Patriarchy, Gender, and the Death of Jezebel." Pages 103–14 in *Take Back the Word: A Queer Reading of the Bible*. Edited by Robert E. Goss and Mona West. Cleveland: Pilgrim.

Koosed, Jennifer L. 2006. "Antimony." *NIDB* 1:178.

Kristeva, Julia. 1982. *Powers of Horror: An Essay on Abjection*. Translated by Leon S. Roudiez. European Perspectives. New York: Columbia University Press.

———. 1991. *Strangers to Ourselves*. Translated by Leon S. Roudiez. New York: Harvester Wheatsheaf.

Kuefler, Mathew. 2001. *The Manly Eunuch: Masculinity, Gender Ambiguity, and Christian Ideology in Late Antiquity*. Chicago: University of Chicago Press.

Lambert, W. G. 1965. "A New Look at the Babylonian Background of Genesis." *JTS* 16:287–300.

Lane, Riki. 2009. "Trans as Bodily Becoming: Rethinking the Biological as Diversity, Not Dichotomy." *Hypatia* 24:136–57.

Leithart, Peter J. 2006. *1 and 2 Kings*. SCM Theological Commentary on the Bible. London: SCM.

Longmore, Paul K. 1997. "Conspicuous Contribution and American Cultural Dilemmas: Telethon Rituals of Cleansing and Renewal." Pages 134–58 in *The Body and Physical Difference: Discourses of Disability*. Edited by David T. Mitchell and Sharon L. Snyder. Ann Arbor: University of Michigan Press.

Lorber, Judith, and Lisa Jean Moore. 2002. *Gender and the Social Construction of Illness*. Plymouth, UK: AltaMira.

Loulan, JoAnne, with Sherry Thomas. 1990. *The Erotic Dance: Butch, Femme, Androgyny, and Other Rhythms*. Minneapolis: Spinsters Ink.

Marble Hornets. 2009. "Entry # 1." YouTube. http://tinyurl.com/SBL0686m.

Martin, Dale B. 1999. *The Corinthian Body*. New Haven: Yale University Press.

Matthews, Victor H. 2006. "Cosmetics." *NIDB* 1:754–55.

McKinlay, Judith E. 2004. *Reframing Her: Biblical Women in Postcolonial Focus*. BMW 1. Sheffield: Sheffield Phoenix.

Meyers, Carol. 1988. *Discovering Eve: Ancient Israelite Women in Context*. Oxford: Oxford University Press.

Minkowitz, Donna. 1994. "Love Hurts." *Village Voice* 19:24–30.

Mollenkott, Virginia Ramey. 2001. *Omnigender: A Trans-religious Approach*. Cleveland: Pilgrim.

Mollenkott, Virginia Ramey, and Vanessa Sheridan. 2003. *Transgender Journeys*. Cleveland: Pilgrim.

Namaste, Viviane K. 2000. *Invisible Lives: The Erasure of Transsexual and Transgender People*. Chicago: University of Chicago Press.

———. 2009. "Undoing Theory: The 'Transgender Question' and the Epistemic Violence of Anglo-American Feminist Theory." *Hypatia* 24:11–32.

Nasrallah, Laura. 2014. "Sacred Meat." *BAR* 40:24, 68.

Nelson, Richard D. 1987. *First and Second Kings.* Interpretation. Atlanta: John Knox.

Niditch, Susan. 1993. *War in the Hebrew Bible: A Study in the Ethics of Violence.* New York: Oxford University Press.

Nissinen, Martti. 1998. *Homoeroticism in the Biblical World: A Historical Perspective.* Translated by Kirsi Stjerna. Minneapolis: Augsburg Fortress.

Nodelman, Perry. 2008. *The Hidden Adult: Defining Children's Literature.* Baltimore: Johns Hopkins University Press.

Novak, Michael Anthony. 2012. "The Odes of Solomon as Apocalyptic Literature." *VC* 66:527–50.

Odelain, O., and R. Séguineau. 1982. *Dictionary of Proper Names and Places in the Bible.* Translated and adapted by Matthew J. O'Connell. London: Robert Hale.

O'Donovan, Oliver. 1982. *Transsexualism and Christian Marriage.* Nottingham: Grove.

Ouro, Roberto. 1999. "The Earth of Genesis 1:2: Abiotic or Chaotic? Part II." *AUSS* 37:39–53.

Parker, Simon B. 1978. "Jezebel's Reception of Jehu." *Maarav* 1:67–78.

Pippin, Tina. 1999. *Apocalyptic Bodies: The Biblical End of the World in Text and Image.* New York: Routledge.

———. 2006. "The Joy of (Apocalyptic) Sex." Pages 64–75 in *Gender and Apocalyptic Desire.* Edited by Brenda E. Brasher and Lee Quinby. London: Routledge.

Prosser, Jay. 1998. *Second Skins: The Body Narratives of Transsexuality.* New York: Columbia University Press.

Provan, Iain W. 1995. *1 and 2 Kings.* NIBCOT. Peabody, MA: Hendrickson.

Raymond, Janice G. 1979. *The Transsexual Empire: The Making of the She-Male.* Boston: Beacon.

Rees, Mark. 1996. "Becoming a Man: The Personal Account of a Female-to-Male Transsexual." Pages 27–38 in *Blending Genders: Social Aspects of Cross-Dressing and Sex-Changing.* Edited by Richard Ekins and Dave King. London and New York: Routledge.

Reeser, Todd W. 2010. *Masculinities in Theory: An Introduction*. Oxford: Wiley Blackwell.

Reynolds, Nancy, and Malcolm McCormick. 2003. *No Fixed Points: Dance in the Twentieth Century*. New Haven: Yale University Press.

Ringe, Sharon H. 1986. "Hospitality, Justice, and Community: Paul's Teaching on the Eucharist." *Prism* 1:59–68.

Rubin, Gayle. 1992. "Of Catamites and Kings: Reflections on Butch, Gender and Boundaries." Pages 466–82 in *The Persistent Desire: A Femme-Butch Reader*. Edited by Joan Nestle. Boston: Alyson.

Rude, Mey. 2014. "Flawless Trans Women Carmen Carrera and Laverne Cox Respond Flawlessly to Katie Couric's Invasive Questions." Autostraddle. http://tinyurl.com/SBL0686g.

Sandelin, Karl-Gustav. 2002. "Drawing the Line: Paul on Idol, Food, and Idolatry in 1 Cor 8:1–11:1." Pages 108–25 in *Neotestamentica et Philonica: Studies in Honor of Peder Borgen*. Edited by David E. Aune, Torrey Seland, and Jarl Henning Ulrichsen. NovTSup 106. Leiden: Brill.

Sanlon, Peter. 2010. *Plastic People: How Queer Theory Is Changing Us*. Latimer Studies 73. London: Latimer Trust.

Savran, George. 1989. "1 and 2 Kings." Pages 146–64 in *The Literary Guide to the Bible*. Edited by Robert Alter and Frank Kermode. London: Fontana.

Sawyer, Deborah F. 2002. *God, Gender and the Bible*. Biblical Limits. London: Routledge.

Scott, Martin. 1992. *Sophia and the Johannine Jesus*. JSNTSup 71. Sheffield: JSOT Press.

Seow, C. L. 1992. "Deep, The." *ABD* 2:125–26.

Serano, Julia. 2007. *Whipping Girl: A Transsexual Woman on Sexism and the Scapegoating of Femininity*. Berkeley: Seal.

Shildrick, Margrit. 2002. *Embodying the Monster: Encounters with the Vulnerable Self*. London: Sage.

"Meetings." n.d. Society of Biblical Literature. http://tinyurl.com/SBL0686k.

Stanley, Ron L. 2006. "Ezra–Nehemiah." Pages 268–77 in *The Queer Bible Commentary*. Edited by Deryn Guest, Bob Goss, Mona West, and Tom Bohache. London: SCM.

Stone, Ken. 2006. "1 and 2 Kings." Pages 222–50 in *The Queer Bible Commentary*. Edited by Deryn Guest, Bob Goss, Mona West, and Tom Bohache. London: SCM.

Stone, Sandy. 1991. "The *Empire* Strikes Back: A Posttranssexual Manifesto." Pages 280–304 in *Body Guards: The Cultural Politics of Gender Ambiguity*. Edited by Julia Epstein and Kristina Straub. New York: Routledge.

Strathern, Marilyn. 1988. *The Gender of the Gift: Problems with Women and Problems with Society in Melanesia*. Berkeley: University of California Press.

Stryker, Susan. 2006. "(De)Subjugated Knowledges: An Introduction to Transgender Studies." Pages 1–17 in *The Transgender Studies Reader*. Edited by Susan Stryker and Stephen Whittle. New York: Routledge.

Sullivan, Nikki. 2003. *A Critical Introduction to Queer Theory*. Edinburgh: Edinburgh University Press.

———. 2006. "Transmogrification: (Un)Becoming Other(s)." Pages 552–64 in *The Transgender Studies Reader*. Edited by Susan Stryker and Stephen Whittle. New York: Routledge.

Sweeney, Deborah. 2011. "Sex and Gender." *UCLA Encyclopedia of Egyptology*. http://escholarship.org/uc/item/3rv0t4np.

Sweeney, Marvin A. 2007. *I and II Kings: A Commentary*. OTL. Louisville: Westminster John Knox.

Tanis, Justin. 2000. "Eating the Crumbs That Fall from the Table: Trusting the Abundance of God." Pages 43–70 in *Take Back the Word: A Queer Reading of the Bible*. Edited by Robert E. Goss and Mona West. Cleveland: Pilgrim.

Thompson, J. A. 1962. "Eye Paint." *IDB* 2:202–3.

Tomes, Roger. 2003. "1 and 2 Kings." Pages 246–81 in *The Eerdmans Bible Commentary*. Edited by James D. G. Dunn and John W. Rogerson. Grand Rapids: Eerdmans.

Trible, Phyllis. 1978. *God and the Rhetoric of Sexuality*. OBT. Philadelphia: Fortress.

———. 1995. "The Odd Couple: Elijah and Jezebel." Pages 166–79 in *Out of the Garden: Women Writers on the Bible*. Edited by Christina Büchmann and Celina Spiegel. London: Pandora.

Tromp, Nicholas J. 1969. *Primitive Conceptions of Death and the Nether World in the Old Testament*. BibOr 21. Rome: Pontifical Biblical Institute.

Tsumura, D. T. 1989. *The Earth and the Waters in Genesis 1 and 2: A Linguistic Investigation*. JSOTSup 83. Sheffield: JSOT Press.

Waldman, Nahum M. 1978. "The Breaking of the Bow." *JQR* 69:82–88.

Waschke, E. J. 2006. "תְּהוֹם." *TDOT* 15:574–81.

Washington, Harold C. 1997. "Violence and the Construction of Gender in the Hebrew Bible: A New Historicism Approach." *BibInt* 5:324–63.

Wenham, Gordon J. 1987. *Genesis 1–15*. WBC 1. Waco, TX: Word Books.

West, Mona. 2006. "Daniel." Pages 427–31 in *The Queer Bible Commentary*. Edited by Deryn Guest, Bob Goss, Mona West, and Tom Bohache. London: SCM.

Westermann, Claus. 1997. "תְּהוֹם." *TDOT* 3:1410–14.

White, Marsha C. 1997. *The Elisha Legends and Jehu's Coup*. BJS 311. Atlanta: Scholars Press.

Whittle, Stephen. 2006. "Foreword." Pages xi–xvi in *The Transgender Studies Reader*. Edited by Susan Stryker and Stephen Whittle. New York: Routledge.

Wilcox, Melissa M. 2009. *Queer Women and Religious Individualism*. Bloomington: Indiana University Press.

Wray Beal, Lissa M. 2007. *The Deuteronomist's Prophet: Narrative Control of Approval and Disapproval in the Story of Jehu (2 Kings 9–10)*. LHBOTS 478. New York: T&T Clark.

Wyatt, Nicolas. 1993. "The Darkness of Genesis I 2." *VT* 43:543–54.

Yeung, Maureen W. 2011. "Boundaries in 'in-Christ Identity': Paul's View on Table Fellowship and Its Implications for Ethnic Identities." Pages 154–74 in *After Imperialism: Christian Identity in China and the Global Evangelical Movement*. Edited by Richard R. Cook and David W. Pao. Eugene, OR: Pickwick.

Zeller, Dieter. 1977. "Die Bildlogik des Gleichnisses Mt. 11 16f/Luke 7 31f." *ZNW* 68: 252–57.

Ancient Sources Index

Author Index

Subject Index

abject, 22, 28, 31–32, 36, 38–43, 50, 65 n. 25, 97–103
Anat, 47 n. 4, 73–74
apocalypse, 11, 98–101, 103
  characteristics of, 99 n. 5
Asherah, 73
bisexual, 2, 14, 38, 48
bodies
  breached, 33, 34
  modification, 34, 39
  "normal," 33, 34
  skin-bound, 33, 34, 55, 82, 83
Christianity,
  fundamentalist, 8, 15
  queer, 17
  transformative, 17
class/classism, 3, 9, 78
cisgender, 39, 42, 57, 68
cissexual, 1, 7, 10–11
  definition, 9
dance, 86
  David's, 88–89
  Greenwich Village movement, 86–87
  Jesus, 91–92
David, king, 11, 19, 61 n. 20, 75, 88, 93
  dancing, 88–89, 93
eunuchs, 18, 19, 47, 58, 72
  Ethiopian, 4, 18
  priests of Cybele, 47 n. 4
feminism, 7, 54, 59 n. 14, 67, 79
  biblical, 22, 31, 70, 78
  radical, 6–9, 18
FTM, 45, 48, 51–53, 59 n. 14, 67, 77, 79
gay, 2, 7, 14, 18, 19, 38, 48, 79

gender
  ambiguity, 11, 18, 22, 35, 36, 48, 52, 55–56, 74, 96, 98–103
  complementarity, 15
  dysphoria, 35
  fluidity, 14–16, 22–23, 45, 51, 77, 79, 88, 101–2
  God-given, 6, 33, 36, 37, 42, 82, 84
  performativity, 29, 46, 47 n. 4, 57, 60, 66, 68, 74, 78, 79
  Recognition Act (UK), 37
  socially constructed, 5, 55 n. 11, 82 n. 1
  transition, 2, 7, 34, 35, 38 n. 8, 46 n. 3, 52, 53, 54, 55, 56, 68, 78, 81, 82, 86, 88, 93, 100, 103
genderism, 38, 40
genderqueer, 10
heteronormativity, 2–4, 11, 22, 41, 43, 48, 49, 51, 54, 67–68, 79
  definition, 9–10, 84–85
heterosexism 4, 5, 9
  definition, 2–3, 84–85
hermeneutics
  of compassion, 33, 43
  ethical responsibility for, 11, 22, 34, 43, 78
  and gender studies, 81 n. 1
intersex, 4, 15, 19, 51
Jehu, 11, 46, 47, 50, 57–79
Jesus, 4, 16, 17, 18, 19, 82, 90–93, 101
Jezebel, 4, 11, 19, 58, 60, 62, 68–77
John, beloved disciple, 16
John the Baptist, 90–91

Lightning Source UK Ltd.
Milton Keynes UK
UKOW03f0035010417
298046UK00001B/68/P